John Buyers is a commercial solicitor and partner at Osborne Clarke LLP, an international law firm which specialises in advising high technology clients, or businesses that are transitioning through a process of digitalisation. John heads Osborne Clarke's international Artificial Intelligence and Machine Learning group and led the UK firm's commercial team for a decade. He is a frequent commentator on the topic of Artificial Intelligence and the law. He speaks, write and records podcasts regularly both in the UK and internationally on the subject.

John's practice is largely based on the licensing and management of machine learning solutions. He regularly advises users and suppliers on regulatory implications and effective monetisation of such solutions. Recent work has included advising a global technology business on automated facial recognition regulation in Europe and on the launch of a new EdTech AI smart speaker.

John is currently advising a US start-up client on the launch of a new LLM generative AI solution.

Artificial Intelligence

The Practical Legal Issues

Third Edition

Artificial Intelligence
The Practical Legal Issues
Third Edition

John C. Buyers, LLB Hons, MA

Solicitor England & Wales

and Republic of Ireland

Partner

Osborne Clarke LLP

Law Brief Publishing

First edition published 2018
Second edition published 2021
This (third) edition published 2023 by Law Brief Publishing, an imprint of Law Brief Publishing Ltd
30 The Parks
Minehead
Somerset
TA24 8BT

www.lawbriefpublishing.com

Paperback: 978-1-916698-14-7

To Nicola

PREFACE

Two years is a very long time in the world of Artificial Intelligence and Machine Learning. The second edition of this book was published in 2021, in the aftermath of the Covid-19 pandemic and initial plans for EU regulation of the technology.

We continue to ride the tidal wave of development, both in terms of regulation and indeed of the technology itself. Since the second edition was published, a new wave of incredibly capable AI tools have been launched on the public – to sentiments equally balanced between excitement and terror.

Generative AI takes the capabilities of the technology to new and dizzying heights and in doing so fundamentally challenges our creative industries and abilities to discern truth from fiction. It is clear that Western democratic society is now polarising into two camps. Those that advocate free market enterprise and the continued exponential development of these technologies and an increasing number of voices (some from very surprising sources) that are advocating a slow down or pause and increased governmental supervision of AI research and development.

Surprisingly the number of industry advocates arguing that the technology has reached "sentience" are also on the rise – one only has to look at the remarkable story of former Google engineer Blake Lemoine who rather extraordinarily made claims to this effect in relation to Google's LaMDA chatbot in mid-2022. Increasingly we will need to address these concerns as AI solutions become more capable and more refined. I suspect however (at least in the short term) that we will be dealing with increasingly sophisticated stochastic parrots (to reiterate a particularly memorable phrase coined by the computational linguist, Emily Bender*)

On the regulatory side, the EU is close to finalisation of its Artificial Intelligence Act and accompanying AI Liability Directive. Post-Brexit, the UK has recently published its own take on AI regulation – the much delayed AI Governance White Paper.

In the USA, the draft federal Algorithmic Accountability Act sits in the House of Representatives and the Biden Presidency has published its "Blueprint for an AI Bill of Rights".

We will examine the legislative trends in more detail later on in this book. Suffice it to say that even though national regulatory mechanisms are different, all roads seem to lead to the concept of an "*AI impact assessment test*". It seems likely that this will be modelled on the data protection impact assessment test of the EU's GDPR.

As is perhaps more than indicated in the book's title, pragmatism and utility for practitioners working in this space has always been my driving philosophy, and I am grateful for the words of praise and encouragement that the first and second editions received. I intend to stick to this mantra.

As I have mentioned in those earlier editions, there will always be books which will delve into these topics in more detail. Mine is intended to be the initial guide into the foothills.

The law in this edition is as stated July 2023. As I have previously indicated, the law on AI and machine learning is a new and emerging field, and there are a number of policy and legislative initiatives which could materially change the analysis in this book.

---

* "*On the Dangers of Stochastic Parrots: Can Language Models be Too Big*" Bender, McMillan-Major, Gebru, Schmitchell, FAccT 21, March 3-10 2021

This book is not intended as a substitute for proper and directed legal advice. In cases of specific query, as ever, please consult with your friendly lawyer.

John C. Buyers
July 2023

ACKNOWLEDGEMENTS

My grateful thanks go to the following people whose helpful thoughts and comments proved invaluable in the preparation of various editions of this work:

Dr Sanjeev B. Ahuja

Catherine Hammon

Evan Lock

CONTENTS

CHAPTER ONE

AN INTRODUCTION TO ARTIFICIALLY INTELLIGENT SYSTEMS

This is a book about technology and artificial intelligence – more specifically one that is designed to assist the non-scientifically minded legal practitioner to understand the implications of this new and exciting technology: to demystify, and hopefully provide clarity around the issues and implications that we as legal practitioners need to take into account when navigating our disparate legal disciplines. It does not purport to be definitive – the technology is far too new for this and is in a state of constant evolution. What it strives to do is to provide a grounding relative to the current "state of the art" as it applies today, and separate fact from fiction.

We are currently experiencing a golden age or renaissance period for machine learning and wider artificial intelligence-based systems. This book is predominantly focussed on the innovations provided by *machine learning* – that is to say technology which, through exponential growth and scale in computing power, has enabled effective use of neural networks to enable machines to adapt and learn *without explicit programming*. It is important however not to ignore associated technologies that complement and enhance machine learning systems, and it is this wider ensemble of techniques (including machine learning itself) which I refer to as *artificial intelligence or AI.*

To the casual observer, it seems that the technology is advancing on a daily or even hourly basis. You can now talk to Alexa or Siri using ordinary spoken words (in whatever language is your norm) and through the miracle of natural language processing get a cogent answer, or instruct

Google to run context based searches on characteristics gleaned from your photo collection. Meta's Facebook will now identify your friends and family for you and Spotify will try to define and predict your musical tastes by selecting music tracks based on your listening history.

Generative AI systems represent the latest explosion in machine learning capability. As we shall see, these types of machine learning systems are capable of generating entirely new content-rich outputs based on simple user text prompts – whether that is in the medium of pictures, via models such as Midjourney or Dall-E, text via OpenAI's ChatGPT, music via GoogleLM or speech synthesis via Uberduck. We are just really beginning to exploit the potential of these technologies.

What makes artificial intelligence systems different from traditional computer systems and why should we be worried?

Sometimes it can be difficult to differentiate fact from fiction – particularly in an environment which is driven by marketing hype and plain old misinformation – especially so given that the idea of the intelligent machine, fuelled by Hollywood, plays heavily on our collective psyche. Is for example artificial intelligence the end of the world as we know it and are we about to be suborned to a new species of supercomputer, or is it the key to a prosperous new future and a golden age of human endeavour? This book will at least give you an oversight of the issues involved from an ethical and legal perspective, and I suspect an appreciation that the reality is somewhat more prosaic than either the pessimists or optimists would have us believe.

In order to understand the practical implications of the technology, it is worth understanding how traditional computer systems work, and analogise this against how neuroscience currently thinks that neurons in the human brain function. We'll then move on and use this analogy to provide a functional explanation for machine learning.

Computers in the traditional sense need prescriptive and directive sets of instructions to execute complex tasks – in essence, their programming. A traditional computer is unable to handle complex tasks effectively unless every eventuality is programmed into its code. As we all know, this makes these machines highly effective at larger repetitive or data intensive tasks, with a defined set of pre-programmed variables. What such machines cannot do well is adapt, learn, evolve or extrapolate their decisions to new and unforeseen situations. In contrast, the human brain although rather less good at repetitive tasks, is a marvel of flexibility and of navigating through a chaotic world. It does this through a process of *conceptualisation.*

The simple act of recognising a human face (or indeed any image) provides a real-life example. You learn from an early age as a human being to recognise a face from any angle or orientation, full on or profile. You can identify someone in low light and you don't need an image of a face to be in colour or even in three dimensions for you to recognise it. Your brain can extrapolate a face from incomplete or partial data – indeed it is unbelievably good at "joining the dots" (so much so that we are often caught out by recognising anthropomorphic features in inanimate objects[1]). A traditionally programmed computer finds this task almost insurmountably complex and difficult to achieve[2]. You need to ensure that the face you want the machine to recognise is oriented in precisely the right way and under precisely the right lighting conditions – as otherwise it may not even identify it as a face. In this context, what the human neo-cortex achieves (and what current AI technologists are trying to replicate) is the holy grail of the "*invariant representation*". This is the ability to learn what a "face" is as a *concept* (or indeed a cube, car, tree or any other animate or inanimate thing) and apply this to real world data. The notion of a concept introduces an entirely new dimension – a level of data abstraction, classification, recognition and labelling which enables

---

1 This is known scientifically as the concept of pareidolia

2 This is difficulty is often referred to as Moravec's Paradox, articulated by Hans Moravec and others in 1988. He postulated that whilst it was comparatively easy to get computers to exhibit "adult" level skills, such as playing chess or checkers (draughts), it was difficult or impossible to give them the skills of a one year-old in terms of perception and mobility

semantic representation in areas such as pattern recognition and linguistics, in short, bringing order from chaos.

Put grandly, artificially intelligent systems aspire through their structures (to a greater or lesser degree) to have the ability to process unstructured data, to extrapolate it, and to adapt and evolve in ways which are comparable to human beings. How they achieve this (as we shall see later) is in fact through the application of deep mathematics, pattern correlation and statistical probabilities.

Robotics, Perception and Artificial Intelligence

So what makes robots different from machine learning systems? It is worth briefly covering the difference as to the uninitiated, this can be a somewhat confusing question – particularly when the terms are used fast, loose and interchangeably in most commercial, non-technical literature.

Obviously, at its most simplistic level, a robot is a mechanism that is designed to replicate the actions and behaviours of living creatures. It is a manufactured autonomous agent in the real world which is capable of autonomous action to a defined degree. Robots in some form or another have been in existence for over 200 years[3].

As AI systems have become more sophisticated and able, robotic research has likewise developed more capable robotic machines and scientists in the field of robotics have become more pre-occupied with replicating animal characteristics of proprioception – the unconscious ability in living creatures of knowing at all times the boundaries and extent of their physical body and that when a limb is extended in front of it, it is part of its own body and has a sense of movement. Knowing also that the limb is sensing hot or cold or touching another object, and whether it is constrained or injured are an integral part of this ability in living creatures. It is this need to physically interact with the real world on an

3 The term robot derives from the Czech word *robota*, which means forced labour or slavery

effective basis which has been described by some commentators as one of the primary catalysts of animal and human intelligence and which is the driving emphasis for AI research in the field of robotics.

A brief history of AI

Before we get into how current "state of the art" artificially intelligent systems are structured, it is worth (briefly) looking at the historical evolution of machine learning. It was Alan Turing who first coined the term "artificial intelligence", and who through his brilliant efforts in the second world war, managed to decode Nazi Germany ciphers produced on the Enigma machine. Alan Turing wrote on the concept of machine intelligence in a seminal 1950 paper[4]. His analysis centred on human intelligence as a benchmark for artificial intelligence (more on this later). He postulated that if you could hold a test where a human conversed with a computer and that human could be fooled by a clever computer program into thinking that the machine they were talking to was in fact human, then the machine would have passed a benchmark for intelligence. This of course evolved into the famous "*Turing test*".

The Turing test led to a surge in the mid-20th century in traditional programming techniques being used to emulate intelligence – however developers very soon realised the limitations of this approach. Programs such as Eliza, one of the very first early winners of a Turing test, fooled reviewers by adopting clever, but simple linguistic tricks (e.g. through the repetition of questions) which gave a superficial semblance of self-awareness and interaction through mimicry but did not create anything approaching human equivalent intelligence. Unsurprisingly AI development stagnated after these initial attempts.

The father of AI is rightly credited to be Marvin Minsky, an American cognitive research scientist who developed the first randomly wired

[4] Computing Machinery and Intelligence (1950) by A.M. Turing

neural network learning machine, SNARC[5] in January 1952. Minsky was also author of the book *Perceptrons* (with Seymour Papert) in 1969 that became a seminal work in the field of artificial neural networks.

For the purposes of this book I am of course paraphrasing a long and complex developmental history – there are many works which espouse the historical evolution of artificial intelligence in a much greater depth but it was subsequent to the development of the Turing test that AI research bifurcated into two distinct directions. One of which centred on the earlier approach of "emulation" – namely focussing on mimicking outwardly observable intelligent behaviours; and a new approach of "simulation" – one which was based on the view that in order to achieve machine intelligence the fundamental structure and processes of neurons firing in the human nervous system had to be simulated.

As we shall see later on, both branches of research are propelling AI development through its current renaissance. There are however still limitations. Not least due to the fact that despite much scientific endeavour, we are still a very long way off from understanding precisely how the human brain functions, and for this reason, even with the advent of generative AI, probably a long way off from developing a machine with human equivalent (or greater) levels of sentience (or feeling, perception and subjective experience), combined with objective reasoning and logic – the holy grail of ***Artificial General Intelligence (AGI)*** or "***Strong AI***".

Inevitably, AI research and development initiatives have themselves evolved and differentiated themselves by trial and error – as some structures have shown promise, those have been refined, so now we have lines of machine learning research and applications which may in fact have very little relationship to how neuroscience currently understands the organisation and structure of the human brain (in addition of course to those that still strive to closely model real organic brain function in so far as it is understood).

5 Stochastic neural analog reinforcement calculator

Current developments

So let's now take a slightly more detailed look at what is actually happening in the field of artificial intelligence at the moment.

As I mentioned at the beginning of this chapter, we have seen a dramatic rise in the effectiveness and use of solutions based on "***Weak AI***" or "***Narrow AI***" or ***Artificial Specific Intelligence (ASI)*** – AI solutions that are based around a specific, narrowly defined task or application, collectively (and somewhat confusingly) falling under the umbrella term of ***IA*** or ***Intelligent Automation.***

Generally speaking, machine learning systems fall into one of four categories – they can be optimised for use cases that involve either *prediction, classification, generation* or *comprehension* (understanding), or obviously any combination of the above:

- *Prediction* refers to the ability of the machine to identify and predict choices;

- *Classification* refers to the ability of the machine to discriminate between different classes of data:

- *Generation* refers to the ability of the machine to generate entirely new classes of data (a particular capability which we will examine in more detail in Chapter Three); and

- *Comprehension* refers to the ability of the machine to understand "real world" inputs, whether that is through text or speech.

Each of the above generally involves different machine learning optimisations and model types. Translating the above categories into use cases, there are several real-world artificial intelligence applications which are driving developments in the technology:

- **Image processing and tagging**

  Image processing as it suggests requires algorithms to analyse images or to discriminate between them to get data or to perform transformations. Facial recognition is the example that immediately springs to mind in this context, however more prosaic examples of this include identification/image tagging – as used in applications such as Facebook to apply name labels to individuals or to ascertain other data from a visual scan, such as health of an individual or location recognition for geodata. Optical Character Recognition – where algorithms learn to read handwritten text and convert documents into digital versions is another good example of this.

- **3D Environment processing**

  3D environment processing is an extension of the image processing and tagging skill – most obviously translated into the skills required by an algorithm in a robot or a "CAV" (connected and autonomous vehicle) to spatially understand its location and environment. This uses image data but also potentially radar and lidar[6] sourced spatial scanning data to process 3D geometries. Typically this technology could also be used in free roaming robot devices including pilotless drones or aisle patrolling robots in supermarkets tasked with reviewing stock levels.

- **Textual Analysis**

  These are techniques and algorithms which extract information from or classify textual data. Textual analysis uses two distinct approaches – one based purely on pattern recognition of words and their meanings and concatenated sequences of the same, the other

6 Lidar measures spatial distances by illuminating objects with laser light and measuring reflections with a sensor. This can then be used to create 3D scans of objects in the immediate vicinity of the CAV

on grammar driven natural language processing. In terms of practical usage, these could include social media postings, tweets or emails. The technology may then be used to provide filtering (for SPAM); information extraction – for example to pull out particular pieces of data such as names and addresses or more complex "sense based" sentiment analysis – to identify the mood of the person writing (as Facebook has recently implemented in relation to postings by members who may be potentially suicidal[7]). Text analysis is also at the heart of Chatbot technology – allowing for interaction on social media, or providing for automated first line technical support.

- **Speech Analysis**

  Speech processing takes equivalent skills to those used for textual documents and applies them to the spoken word. It is this area which is seeing an incredible level of investment in the creation of personal digital home assistants from the likes of Amazon (with its Echo device), Google's Home device and Apple with Siri. As with textual analysis, speech analysis has moved into a more sophisticated realm of understanding not just the words themselves, but also the manner in which they are spoken. Emotion detection tools are now playing a key part in back office call centre SLA management[8].

- **Data Mining**

  This is the process of discovering patterns or extrapolating trends from data. Data mining algorithms are used for such things as Anomaly detection – identifying for example fraudulent entries or

7 See for example http://www.bbc.co.uk/news/technology-39126027 "Facebook artificial intelligence spots suicidal users", 1st March 2017

8 See for example Deloitte's TrueVoice software enterprise product. TrueVoice applies behaviour and emotion analytics to assist in the optimal management of call centres

transactions as outliers or classifying them as known types of fraud; Association rules – detecting supermarket purchasing habits by looking at a shopper's typical shopping basket; and Predictions – predicting a variable from a set of others to extrapolate for example a credit score.

- **Video game virtual environment processing**

  Video games are a multi-billion dollar entertainment industry but they are also key sandboxes for machines to interact with and learn behaviours in relation to other elements in a virtual environment, including interacting with the players themselves[9].

Machine Learning – Understanding the basic elements

At the most simplistic level, machine learning systems are no different from conventional computer systems in that both rely on the elements of computational hardware and software to function effectively.

Whilst many modern machine learning systems exploit huge advances in computing scale and power and make use of the vast amounts of data that are available in our "big data" society, they still need what would be recognisable as a computing platform. It is the logic or software that such systems use which differs markedly from traditional computer programs directly created by human programmers which require sequential, explicit and largely linear instructions that are followed to the letter by the machine.

I have already explained that technologists developing machine learning systems have developed a variety of solutions, methodologies, models and structures to get machines to "*think*" in a narrow AI sense. In fact so many

9 See for example the August 2017 edition knowledge feature of Edge Magazine – "Machine Language" which discusses new startup SpiritAI – a business that has developed an intelligent character engine for NPCs (non-player characters) in video games, thus obviating the need for thousands of pages of pre-scripted dialogue

approaches have been developed, it can be difficult for the non-computer scientist to effectively decode them. To further complicate this issue, many proprietary machine learning systems employ a "mix" of adaptive learning solutions which are optimised for the particular applications at hand. We'll step through some of these models in a moment, but for the moment, and in order to provide a consistent framework for you, the reader, it is worth setting out the very basic absolutes of machine learning systems – in other words, those conceptual elements that ***all*** current machine learning systems use. It is important to stress that this framework applies to that subset of AI which is *machine learning* as defined at the beginning of this chapter – the terms may not be relevant to other wider or peripheral AI technologies which are generally out of scope for the purposes of this book.

At the most simplistic level It is generally established that machine learning systems are comprised of three parts: the ***Model*** – that is to say the way in which the system is structured and organised – in short its mathematical architecture, including the nodes, links and weights which will be applied to the data to be processed. Then there are the ***Parameters*** – these are the properties of the training data that are to be learned during training and finally the ***Learner*** –generally comprised of a ***learning algorithm*** – that part of the system that adjusts the model for how it processes the parameters on a *supervised, unsupervised* or *reinforcement* basis (see below under "*Training*") and an ***activation or transfer algorithm*** which defines the way in which data are to be transferred between nodes within the network by forwards and or backwards propagation (see further below under "*Backpropagation*").

Algorithms

The word "***algorithm***" is often used to generalise the entire process I have described above. In many texts you might as well substitute the words for "*magic spell*".

In fact, as we have seen above, an algorithm is merely a set of complex mathematical actions expressed as a formula conceptualising the model utilised by the system. Clearly machine learning algorithms are not magic spells. More prosaically, learning algorithms selectively adapt and change the model and parameters based on the data that is introduced into the machine learning system. Rather confusingly as well, it is important to note (and often misunderstood), that simply referring to a solution that is "*algorithmic*" does not necessarily imply that that solution has any degree of artificial intelligence or machine learning.

Training

All machine learning systems need to be "***trained***" (or train themselves) with a data set – a set of data points which are intended to assist the system to "understand" the relevant narrow AI task at hand and which contain the parameters I have described above. Training data sets are, as we shall see later on in this book, an incredibly significant and important feature of these systems. The nature of the training data set provided however is very different depending upon whether the system is designed to learn on a "***supervised***", "***unsupervised***" or "***reinforcement***" basis.

Supervised Learning

Supervised learning systems are provided with guiding or labelled training data sets that contain a mass of examples of the desired answers and outputs. In such cases, the training data are subsets of data that are well known in terms of all of their features, content, correlations and so forth and thus can provide a good representative example to benchmark the outputs of the system. Typically these data sets will be past, real life examples of the problem the system has been configured to resolve. Usually this type of machine learning supports evaluation, classification or prediction outcomes.

Unsupervised Learning

Systems that are designed to learn on an unsupervised basis in contrast are provided with unlabelled data that may or may not contain the desired answer or output. In these cases, the systems attempt to find either outliers or correlations or patterns in the data without any form of guidance.

Provided data sets may be clustered into different classes that share some common characteristics – unsurprisingly, this is often referred to as "*clustering*" by the industry. As we'll see in Chapter Three, Generative AI tools use innovative variations of this type of learning (typically on a massive scale), to generate novel outputs.

Reinforcement Learning

Reinforcement learning is a similar process to unsupervised learning – however machine learning systems here are typically exposed to a rules-based competitive environment where they train themselves continuously using trial and error to try to find the best reward – which might be winning a game or earning more money. This type of AI system attempts to learn from past experience in order to refine and improve decision outcomes, and is particularly well suited to closed environments with a static framework.

Whether the system is designed to work on a supervised or unsupervised basis it is clearly vitally important that the data sets provided to train the system need to be representative of the underlying problem the system is being designed to resolve and should not be unbalanced or skewed in any particular direction (aka *biased*). As we'll see later on in this book, there are particular issues with this which could trap the unwary. Proactively editing out bias too far in a data set may well have the opposite and undesired effect of making that data set too specific (so called "*overfitting*") and less representative of the data class, in turn leading to the corresponding outputs of the system being prejudiced in favour of or against particular outcomes.

Backpropagation

Backpropagation is the process which allows a machine learning system to adjust and change by reference to previous outcomes.

In technical terms it is the means by which the machine learning system (via the *activation algorithm*, see above) mathematically computes and optimises the gradient descent required in the calculation of weights used in the network by distributing *back* through network nodes.

So these are the basic features of AI or machine learning systems. As I mentioned above, there are a variety of different AI ***Models*** which are being deployed, and it is worth spending a little time on the most significant of these.

Artificial Neural Networks

Artificial neural networks aim to most closely model the functioning of the human brain through the simulation approach and contain all of the basic machine learning elements described above.

Neuroscience has established that the human neo-cortex, which is where most of our higher brain function resides, consists of a very dense population of interconnected neurons or brain cells. Neurons consist of the soma (the cell body) and axons and dendrites (the filaments that extend from the cell itself). Observed higher human brain functions require groups or networks of neurons to fire together in electro chemical activity. Even though the base physical structure of the cortex is the same, it is settled science that there are cortical regions that specialise in particular skills, such as language, motor movement, sight and hearing. More recently, it has been established that there are progressively "higher" levels of brain processing driven by layers of neurons. You might for example have a collection of neurons at a low level that are specialised in the visual detection of "edges". Data from these lower functions is passed up the tree (or network) to higher functions, such as those that might detect nose shapes or eye shapes, so that collectively, you are able to perceive a face[10].

---

10 Bizarrely, scientist have apparently discovered that there is a neuron that appears to be dedicated to Bill Clinton recognition. See *On Intelligence*, by Jeff Hawkins

In the world of artificial intelligence, scientists have attempted to replicate or model these structures and their functionality by use of neural networks. In simplistic terms, neural networks can be organised as "shallow" – 1-3 layers or "deep" – over 7 layers (as is generally the case in the human neo-cortex).

Artificial neural networks are composed of artificial input "neurons" – virtual computing "cells" that *activate*, that is to say, assume a numeric value (by reference to a chosen algorithm which applies weights and biases to that numeric value – in effect influencing it) and then hand it off to another layer of the network, which also applies an algorithmic treatment to it, and so on and so forth until the data has passed through the entire network and is outputted.

The process is heavily mathematical. Most neural networks apply something called a *cost function*, which is an additional mathematical process that determines how to adjust the network's weights and biases in order to make it more accurate. Typically this is achieved by something called *gradient descent* – a calculus derived mathematical function which is designed to reach the *minima* (the lowest possible, and hence the most accurate value, of the *cost function* described above).

Stepping away from the maths for a moment, it is worth making the point that Artificial Neural Networks process data in a highly complex non-linear manner through a number of 'hidden layers' – as we saw from the basic elements section above, data may *backpropagate* as well as move forwards through the network (a further mathematically driven process of output refinement and tuning). This complexity drives opacity in their processes which often leads them to being referred to as "*black boxes*". This can make it very difficult to understand and equally difficult to explain how or why the system has reached a particular outcome in a particular instance.

It is also important to note that neural networks come in a variety of flavours, so for example ***Regression Neural Networks*** are neural networks that are trained to analyse data on either a linear or non-linear regression basis (a simple example of regression analysis might be extrapolating growth rates from height measurements taken from a child).

Deep Learning Networks

Deep learning models are simply varieties of artificial neural networks that employ vastly greater computing power, more recent algorithmic innovations and much bigger data sets – in short, they take advantage of the much greater computing power available to us, but operate in much the same manner as I have described above. Of course, the challenges of explainability and transparency are also correspondingly amplified when such networks are used.

On a wider basis, it is probably worth providing a brief introduction to some other non-machine learning AI technologies, although I do not propose to delve into these in any great detail.

Decision Trees

In contrast to machine learning, decision trees are a "*white box*" artificial intelligence model – typically their decisions are more easily explicable and they are principally used for classification style problems. In simple terms a decision tree works by processing data through a series of question "nodes" (similar to a flow diagram type structure). Each node hands off data to corresponding next layer once a question has been answered. Decision trees usually work on a Boolean basis (ie *yes* or *no*).

Decision trees depend upon being able to classify data sets in an expected manner and are not suitable for applications that are based on unsupervised pattern correlation or recognition. This means that they are in turn susceptible to in-built bias if the overall problem they are designed to resolve has been incorrectly modelled.

Random Forests

Random Forests and Deep Forests are very large ensembles of Decision Trees. In simple terms, Random Forests take random subsets of data to be analysed and assign these to individual trees. The collective output of the trees provides a range of responses which can be correlated on a statistical basis to provide a stronger prediction than a single decision tree alone. I do not propose to explain the intricacies of these structures further in this book, however the reader should note that by aggregating decision trees together in a very large hierarchy, such structures may become inherently less explicable in terms of their decision making.

Probabilistic artificial intelligence

Probabilistic or Bayesian artificial intelligence techniques are some of the hardest to conceptualise and understand. They may or may not incorporate machine learning technology. Systems that work on this basis are attempting, by application of mathematical probability theory, to express all forms of uncertainty associated with the problem the model is trying to resolve. They then apply inverse probability (***Bayes' Rule***) to infer unknown characteristics of the problem to make predictions about, and learn from, observed data (so called "***inference algorithms***").

The greatest strength of Probabilistic models is that they *know what they do not know* or in effect have an internal representation of past outcomes that are learned, on the basis of which they can guess a probable outcome. We live and work in a very messy world – and many decisions we take are inferred from observable data sets that are incomplete. Such systems are therefore incredibly powerful but do depend on a very careful probabilistic representation of uncertainty.

So that was an introduction to the key elements of the technology. In the following chapter we delve into a little more detail on the core ethical issues surrounding the use and deployment of machine learning systems (as these ethical issues form the keystone of nascent AI regulation). In Chapter Three we discuss the latest and most controversial aspects of the technology, Generative AI, and explain how that differs from what I would refer to as the established AI techniques discussed in this chapter.

CHAPTER TWO

AI ETHICS:
A PRIMER

As I explained in Chapter One, a basic understanding of AI Ethics is necessary to understand the concern of legislators formulating regulation in this area and to give a wider appreciation of where such legislation may ultimately end up.

Such a discussion is particularly apposite in the current climate when much commentary has been fuelled by generative AI. This chapter sets out those ethical building blocks, on a high-level introductory basis[11].

Beneficial Purpose

One of the key principles relating to AI and which is much discussed in ethical circles is the extent to which any such usage of the technology is directed towards a beneficial purpose for society. In essence, this is a manifestation of the original "*don't be evil*" mantra coined by Google as part of its corporate code of conduct[12].

Artificial Intelligence has demonstrated itself as an incredibly capable and transformative technology. In fact, as we are all aware and as I explained in Chapter One, this capability is not static but is on a path of near linear

---

[11] There are of course innumerable publications on AI Ethics which will further guide the reader. I would in particular however highly recommend the OECD's AI Principles (available at See https://oecd.ai/en/ai-principles) and "*Responsible AI: A Global Policy Framework*", initially published 2019 but subsequently updated in 2021 which is a leading publication produced by a community of international lawyer members of the International Technology Law Association and available on their website www.itechlaw.org

[12] This was replaced by "*do the right thing*" following the Google restructuring under Alphabet, Inc. in 2015

progression.

In part then, this '*beneficial purpose*' principle is a reflection of the potential for immense harm and disruption to society that the technology could cause if it is misused (or at the very least indiscriminately used without thought for the consequences involved). It is also an ethical principle which is likely to come progressively sharply into focus as the technology becomes more and more capable.

There are of course many areas which could be impacted by this ethical principle, but for the purposes of this primer I propose to illustrate a few of the more important ones.

- **Human Autonomy**

  The first area which is worth considering is the potential for the technology to undermine human autonomy (that is to say an individual's capacity for self-determination and self-governance) and remove essential elements of trust from society by making it difficult if not impossible to distinguish what is real from what is fake. We are already in a sense seeing this manifesting with increasingly sophisticated "*deep fakes*" (many powered by generative AI).

  Additionally, the capability of such systems to manipulate data sources and create disinformation on a sophisticated basis may have already played a role in alleged election interference in several democratic countries and its use in such contexts is only likely to increase[13]. Ultimately not being able to discern what is real pulls apart the threads of democratic society.

---

13 See for example "*Microsoft economist warns of A.I. election interference from 'bad actors'*" CNBC.com May 3, 2023 https://www.cnbc.com/2023/05/03/microsoft-economist-warns-of-ai-bad-actors-meddling-with-elections.html

- **The Future of Work**

  The second area is of course the potential for these technologies to automate jobs and undermine employment (or indeed to transform them into less attractive, uninteresting roles). This is not a new issue – throughout previous industrial revolutions we have seen the capacity of machines to automate jobs which were previously done by humans. The difference here perhaps is that AI takes this to new extremes. Previously machines were only capable of automating the most mechanical of tasks. Now AI, especially with generative systems, is encroaching on the preserve of creative workers. Writers and artists are in the forefront of this transformation[14], but it does not take much imagination to see that being extended across to the professions, such as law, accountancy and medicine.

- **Lethal Autonomous Weapons**

  Understandably weapons that have the ability to take human life or "LAWs" sit at the pinnacle of ethical use considerations. The simple expression of ethical use in this context is that machines should not be permitted to take irreversible and autonomous "kill decisions" in the absence of an active human in the decision loop. Campaigners in civil society have voiced strong concerns at the development of these technologies[15].

  The United Nations has convened a group of governmental experts

---

14 Indeed the WGA (Writer's Guild of America) has recognised this and has gone on strike in part to restrict the use of generative AI in the writing of film and TV scripts. See "*Why use of AI is a major sticking point in the ongoing writers' strike*" New Scientist, May 2023 https://www.newscientist.com/article/2373382-why-use-of-ai-is-a-major-sticking-point-in-the-ongoing-writers-strike/

15 See for example the Campaign to stop Killer Robots, a coalition of 200 individuals and NGOs that seek to outlaw the use of such technology (www.stopkillerrobots.org)

on an ongoing basis to review the impact of LAWs within the wider context of weapons considered to be "excessively injurious" or having indiscriminate effects[16]. Some UN member states have aligned their defence codes of conduct to this review as well as formulating ethical principles which are consistent with a policy of "humans first"[17].

Accountability

The debate on lethal autonomous weapons neatly segues into the second key ethical principle which is critical to an understanding of AI ethics – that of Accountability. In fundamental terms, this principle requires a party to hold accountability for the decisions made by AI systems.

A few years ago the debate centred on whether it was possible to give such machines legal personality and hence hold them directly accountable[18]. This line of thinking however has fortunately been widely discredited and most contemporary effort is focussed on the best way to make humans fully accountable for such autonomous decisions: whether this is at the outset of the decision-making process; during it; after it has been made or ultimately overseeing it.

---

16 See the UN Convention on Certain Conventional Weapons (CCW), in particular review document CCW CONF II 2-E (https://treaties.un.org/doc/source/docs/CCW_CONF_II_2-E.pdf)

17 See for example the UK Ministry of Defence publication "*Ambitious, safe, responsible: our approach to the delivery of AI-enabled capability in Defence*", available at https://www.gov.uk/government/publications/ambitious-safe-responsible-our-approach-to-the-delivery-of-ai-enabled-capability-in-defence/ambitious-safe-responsible-our-approach-to-the-delivery-of-ai-enabled-capability-in-defence

18 See the EU Parliament's recommendation on granting legal status to AI and robots to the *Commission on Civil Law Rules on Robotics*, 2017 (further discussed in Chapter Four on Causation. Since this report however the EU parliament has considered the application of what are referred to as "*electronic personalities*" on a more discriminating, case by case basis. See the 2020 Study on *Artificial Intelligence and Civil Liability*: https://www.europarl.europa.eu/RegData/etudes/STUD/2020/621926/IPOL_STU(2020)621926_EN.pdf

Clearly these ethical accountability issues become harder to resolve when machine decisions are made at scale or at a speed which would make meaningful human involvement difficult to incorporate. In particular, there will be cases where providing humans in the decision-making loop could completely obviate the financial use case of the technology in the first place.

Transparency and Explainability

As I explain in Chapter One and more fully in Chapter Four on Causation, machine learning systems are inherently opaque in their operation – colloquially referred to as "*black boxes*". In particular with deep neural networks, even though data scientists can create algorithmic models to undertake particular tasks, *they still do not understand in any particular given situation how or why a system came to the conclusion that it did.*

AI systems effectively parse datasets in order to reach "decisions" – typically statistical correlations – in relation to such data. These decisions are a product of their mathematical model. Unlike traditional computer programs which are a direct sequence of linear instructions and which produce predictable results, the outputs of a machine learning system tend (as with humans making a decision) to be distributed along a probability curve. Some such decisions are within the apex of such a curve and therefore "predictable" or "usual" to a degree, others sit on the margins of the curve (so called "*edge case decisions*") and are less predictable. The upshot of this discussion is that with opaque machine learning systems, *you sometimes get what you are not looking for*[19].

This principle was rather well illustrated by the case of Mount Sinai Hospital, which in 2017 deployed an advanced AI system called "Deep Patient" to review the records of some 700,000 patients. What the hospital found was that Deep Patient became adept at diagnosing adult schizophrenia (or at least the likelihood that individuals would develop

[19] A quotation from Alexander Fleming, the discoverer of Penicillin

that condition), but they had no idea how the system had developed that capability[20].

This lack of transparency or opaqueness also creates particular issues in a regulatory sense where such machines are required to make decisions which have significant consequences on the individuals involved, whether that is through the denial of credit; a failure to be recruited or promoted or a decision denying individual liberty, society dictates that such decisions should be capable of challenge. These are concerns that have been picked up by European regulators in the context of the GDPR under Article 22 on Automated Decision making (see Chapter Six for a further discussion) and to a degree are carried into the EU's new Artificial Intelligence Act draft (see Chapter Five).

Alongside these particular transparency concerns, ethical use of AI systems requires that not only should users have sufficient explanation or instructions on how such systems should be used properly, they should also understand how they work, and what the consequences might be for their usage. These are not insignificant challenges for regulators but it is clear that whether or not the draft regulation is the EU Artificial Intelligence Act, the US Algorithmic Accountability Act or the UK's approach to AI governance, the use of impact assessments in determining these considerations on a contextual basis will be a consistent feature and particularly critical.

Safety

Transparency and explainability have a particularly close relationship to the next ethical principle which is that of safety. This is because having a full understanding of how something works and how it might react in any given situation is critical to determining how safe that system actually

20 See "*Deep Learning: The Most Advanced Artificial Intelligence*" – Chris Brandt, Mount Sinai University Herald – https://www.mountsinai.org/about/newsroom/2017/university-herald-deep-learning-the-most-advanced-artificial-intelligence-chris-brandt

is.

Predictability of response is also vitally important in applications which may have a real impact on physical safety such as autonomous driving and piloting systems. As I am sure you are aware following our discussion of the transparency and explainability principles earlier, this is a potential concern in relation to systems that are prone to unpredictability in their responses or decisions[21].

Notwithstanding this issue – it is clear that AI systems used in safety critical applications also need to be robust in their operation and should be fully specified. This also includes the ability of such systems to "hand over" control to human operators or users in a graceful manner in a fallback situation[22].

Absence of Bias (fairness)

Fairness – or the absence of bias is another key ethical principle which is important to take into account when using and deploying AI systems. This is because such systems are heavily dependent upon the training data sets that are fed into them.

When training such systems it is important to ensure that the data used

---

21 This issue was brought to life by a recent issue with the AI MCAS autopilot system fitted to Boeing's 737 Max aircraft. In 2019 two airliners crashed, one operated by Ethiopian Air and the other by Lion Air. It is thought that the pilots struggled to take control of the aircraft from the autopilot – which was confused by faulty sensor data – see *"How a 'confused' AI may have fought pilots attempting to save Boeing 737 MAX8s"* https://www.news.com.au/technology/innovation/inventions/how-a-confused-ai-may-have-fought-pilots-attempting-to-save-boeing-737-max8s/news-story/bf0d102f699905e5aa8d1f6d65f4c27e#:~:text=Pilots%20would%20have%20no%20idea,attemping%20to%20over%2Dride%20it.

22 For a wider discussion of safety issues in AI please see *Key Concepts in AI Safety: An Overview*, published 2021 by the Center for Security and Emerging Technology – https://cset.georgetown.edu/wp-content/uploads/CSET-Key-Concepts-in-AI-Safety-An-Overview.pdf

is not "*overfitted*" – that is to say no overt or covert biases are introduced to skew the decision making capability of the machine. As the data scientists managing Google translate have discovered, machine learning systems tend to re-iterate the biases of materials used in the system training process. If that includes texts, such as the bible, which are thousands of years old, you can inadvertently end up introducing ancient cultural prejudice into modern outputs[23].

Privacy

The ethical principle of privacy reflects the fact that machine learning systems, given their extraordinary capabilities, can, when used in particular applications, severely constrain the ability of individuals to freely enjoy their lives in the absence of surveillance and monitoring.

This right to privacy is enshrined in Article 8 of the European Convention of Human Rights[24]. The right to privacy is not explicitly referenced in the US constitution per se but there is a long evolved and established precedent supporting such rights in the US[25].

Open access vs. proprietary rights

Finally, it is worth mentioning that there is a continuing and ongoing tension between making such systems openly available and exercising proprietary (intellectual) rights over them.

The ethical principle is simple – and broadly analogous to that supporting availability of generic medicines. It runs that systems that

---

23 I discuss this in more detail in Chapter Nine on Automated Bias and Discrimination

24 Article 8 of the ECHR provides a right to respect "*for one's private and family life, his home and his correspondence*", subject to certain constraints. See https://www.echr.coe.int/documents/d/echr/Guide_Art_8_ENG

25 Generally inferred by the US Supreme court indirectly via reference to other constitutional documents and amendments, including the Bill of Rights and the 1st, 3rd, 4th, 9th and 14th Amendments

could have a step-change in societal improvement should be made available to all. Obviously the counter argument is that those who have invested considerable resources and efforts in their development should be entitled to reap the economic returns of their deployment. This tension is in fact being played out in the current AI market, which is bifurcated into traditional "closed source" enterprise led models by the SaaS majors, such as AWS and Azure, and a more open-source style model driven by the MLOps markets hosted by GitHub and Linux Foundation[26].

[26] For a fuller discussion see Chapter Twelve AI and Automated Service Provision

CHAPTER THREE

GENERATIVE AI SYSTEMS

On November 30th 2022 OpenAI launched its AI chatbot ChatGPT onto an unsuspecting public, and in doing so unleashed a wave of commentary unprecedented even in the much commented upon AI space.

What made ChatGPT particularly noteworthy was the step change of improvement it represented in terms of human interaction, as well as the fact that it was suddenly accessible by everyone on an ostensibly "free" egalitarian basis.

Suddenly members of the public were able to log onto a publicly available website, type questions into a text-based interface and receive rich, detailed and human-like responses.

ChatGPT has been followed by a slew of similar Generative AI tools in the last six months.

Such levels of interaction have fuelled the public consciousness and desire for intelligent machines. In many cases this has caused the less well informed to become victims of their own "*automation bias*", that is to say, the tendency of humans to take at face value and accept the outputs of such machines[27].

---

[27] In a recently publicised case, Samsung engineers used generative AI tool AI Writer to generate system code for products in development, as well as entering details of unreleased confidential products and internal notes as prompts into ChatGPT. See https://www.techradar.com/news/samsung-workers-leaked-company-secrets-by-using-chatgpt

Notwithstanding Generative AI systems constituting machine learning systems (as we discussed in Chapter One), due to the way in which they are trained and made available for use they present their own unique risks which are worth discussing in a separate chapter.

Generative AI systems share certain characteristics but rely on different machine learning techniques in order to achieve their particular novel content outputs: whether that is image, text, voice or music synthesis.

At the time of writing, there are a number of such tools but inevitably this landscape is highly fluid and is only likely to expand, change and develop. The techniques used are also complex and mathematical, so in order to make the explanations accessible to non-data scientists, I have inevitably conceptualised them into high-level characterisations.

Machine learning models have traditionally relied on what is referred to as discriminative modelling in order to process the data they are trained on. This type of technique tries to classify input data and attempts to predict, using mathematical probabilities, what that data is based on features which distinguish the chosen class from other data elements. A simple example might be to classify and distinguish bedrooms from other rooms in a house by identifying a bed "feature" in images of such rooms. Other features might indicate the room is a bedroom (but have a lower probability) such as the presence of curtains.

The latest cohort of generative AI tools have moved away from these traditional techniques and now rely on a variety of optimised machine learning models that typically enable scraping of very large amounts of data on an unsupervised basis, without relying on the laborious process of labelling data elements. Below I explain how some of the more popular models work. Again, I should stress that these models are heavily mathematical, and based on statistical probabilities.

Generative Adversarial Networks (or "GANs")

Convolutional Neural Networks or ("CNNs") have a structure which is specifically optimised for image recognition (such networks assume that all inputs are image related). Generative Adversarial Networks ("GANs") take this one step further and improve applications such as image recognition and optimisation by pitting one CNN against another.

One network acts as image generator, the other acts as image discriminator, challenging the generating network to improve its output. Use of this technique has proved very valuable in picture enhancement – such as for example improving the resolution of fuzzy long range satellite images or removing artefacts.

GANs are also particularly effective where no correlated data exists to underpin decisions relating to a processing application – in other words, unlike the discriminative models we just discussed, they can be used to synthesise data where none actually exist. OpenAI's first generation Dall-E is an examples of generative image systems that uses GANs to create outputs.

Normalising Flow Models

Normalising Flow models can be conceptualised in their operation as pushing an initial data density through a series of transformations to produce a richer, more complex distribution – in the manner of fluid flowing through tubes. These "flows" can be applied to generative and predictive modelling[28]. The Google Pixel 4 phone uses Flow modelling in its image manipulation toolset.

---

[28] See Andrej Karpathy, "*What are Normalising Flows and Why Should We care*", Analytics India Magazine. Available at: https://analyticsindiamag.com/what-normalising-flows-machine-learning-deepmind-google-ai/

Diffusion Models

Diffusion models are currently regarded as superior to GANs in the generation of images. This is because typically they are not prone to some of the computational weaknesses of GANs.

Diffusion models draw inspiration from statistical and thermodynamic physics by noting that any localised distribution of particles will eventually spread out to fill an entire space evenly through random diffusion. These models work by degrading training images with random (gaussian) noise so that they end up being completely disintegrated. The machine learning model then in essence is trained step by step to progressively work backwards, reversing this disruption so that it can successfully predict a de-noised image version from the previous one, ultimately creating a novel image that is similar (but not identical to) the initial training image.

Some of the more innovative image generative AI models such as Midjourney and Stable Diffusion use this technique.

Transformer Models

Transformers (or more colloquially, LLMs or large language models) are deep neural networks that learn context and meaning by tracking relationships in sequential data – such as words in a sentence. These models are typically pre-trained in an unsupervised manner and then "fine-tuned" using supervised training to refine their outputs.

Transformers work via multiple encoder and decoder elements. The encoder examines the input text sequence, extracts all of the features within it and converts them into vectors (representations of the position and semantics of a word in a sentence). It then then hands off to the decoder element.

The decoder works on target outputs, in effect predicting the next word in an output sequence. Typically these models have many "blocks" of encoders and decoders that work on multiple progressive sequences. This encode-decode iterative relationship is also referred to as an *attention* or *self-attention* mechanism and enables the transformer to directly model relationships between all of the words in a sentence (ie all of the relevant data vectors), regardless of where they are located.

Some well-known examples of transformer models include OpenAI's Chat-GPT3 and Google's LaMDA.

So, given the nature of these generative AI tools, what then are the specific issues that you need to be mindful on a pragmatic basis when providing advice on their use?

Configuration and Release of Generative AI models

Understanding how such generative AI models are generally brought to market is essential to contextualise some of the real issues around their usage.

Most publicly available generative AI models go through an initial pre-release or configuration stage, where they are subjected to a form of unsupervised training that usually encompasses significant web-scraping on the part of the developer. This "configuration model" as I refer to it is then launched as a "release model" which can be accessed by users via text prompts or APIs that enable it to generate specific outputs. In some cases the user-generated text prompts are utilised for further training and refinement of the "configuration model".

This is the case for example with tools such as OpenAI's Chat-GPT (in the context of text synthesis), and Midjourney (in the context of image synthesis).

Developers such as OpenAI are very circumspect about the amount of data used to train their tools, and indeed their sources, however informed opinion has estimated that Chat-GPT3 was trained on between 45-60 terabytes of web scraped data – which is roughly equivalent to one million feet of physical bookshelf space. Sources are likely to have included Wikipedia, Discord, Reddit and Google[29].

Intellectual Property Issues

We specifically discuss AI and IP issues in detail in Chapter Eight. In so far as generative AI models are concerned, and aside from the more detailed considerations raised in that chapter, there are two specific IP issues that you need to be mindful of.

The first is understanding how intellectual property rights in the input datasets used to train the configuration model have been handled. There are copyright law issues at play here, as in most jurisdictions, simply scraping internet data because it is publicly available does not necessarily mean that the relevant licensor has agreed to it being used for the purpose of training a machine learning model[30].

If scraping such data is not permissible under law then the proprietor of that model may be subject to copyright enforcement proceedings for undertaking such activity. This is precisely the issue at hand in relation to two sets of separate ongoing litigation lawsuits.

The first case is between Getty Images and Stability AI[31]. Getty initiated proceedings against Stability AI, the proprietors of generative AI tool Stable Diffusion, in both the USA and UK alleging that it misused more

29 See for example "*ChatGPT User Statistics & Facts*", https://seo.ai/blog/chatgpt-user-statistics-facts

30 A proposed amendment to the UK Copyright regime following on from a 2021 UK Intellectual Property Office consultation and review to allow for a new text and data mining exception in relation to copyright and data base rights "*for any reason*" has been heavily criticised in the House of Lords, and may, at the time of writing now not be implemented

31 *Getty Images (US), Inc. vs. Stability AI, Inc.* filed 3rd Feb 2023, Case 1:23-cv-00135-UNA in the US District Court, Delaware District

than 12 million Getty images in the process of training its model[32].

The lawsuit was filed in the UK in February 2023 and subsequently in Delaware in the US and the courts in both jurisdictions are yet to reach a judgment.

In a similar vein a number of litigants have joined in a class action against the providers of CoPilot, a generative AI coding tool[33]. The difference in this case however is that the complaint alleges a failure on the part of the defendants to attribute authorship of various open-source code elements used in training the model, in accordance with the open-source licenses governing the use of such coding elements.

The second intellectual property issue relative to generative AI in particular is determining what intellectual property rights you have in the generative outputs of such AI tools.

As we have just seen, if in fact the scraping activity carried out as part of the model training process is carried out in breach of copyright in licensed works (in the absence of a valid licensing arrangement or legitimate statutory exception, such as fair use or fair dealing) then in theory any output derived from such data could also in fact be infringing, rendering the user potentially subject to infringement proceedings.

In practical terms, at the time of writing, the two determinative cases mentioned are still being considered. Clearly such wholesale and massive web scraping activity represents a threat to conventional copyright licence rights holders and this case goes right to the heart of whether such activity does in fact constitute copyright infringement.

---

32 There were relatively strong indicators that Getty's image library had been used as there were clear instances of Stable Diffusion images regenerating the Getty Image watermark as part of generated outputs

33 *Butterick, Manfredi & Zirpoli vs. GitHub, Microsoft, OpenAI* filed 3rd November 2022, Case 3:22-cv-0683 in the US District Court, Northern California, San Francisco Division

The third issue which may be related to intellectual property is understanding and being able to control the degree to which your own inputs into the release model are used to train the configuration model. Whether this is a significant issue will depend of course on the context – in particular what inputs are being entered, and whether these themselves are subject to copyright (and the degree to which you wish them to be protected). Aside from intellectual property, there are clear confidentiality and (as we shall see shortly) data protection issues involved when typing information into generative AI systems that is itself confidential or constitutes personal data.

Clearly, when any use of generative AI is being contemplated, the duty is on legal advisors to get visibility from providers as to the data sources being used to train underlying configuration models and to the extent possible, confirmation that either appropriate licence terms have been agreed or that the relevant training materials are not subject to copyright. This of itself is a non-trivial task when dealing with the massive scale of data sets used to train such systems (which are getting larger and larger with each technological iteration) and may not be achievable, especially in a climate where such providers are less than candid about the sources used to train their models.

In so far as your own inputs into these systems are concerned (whether they be text, images, sound or music) you will need to understand how and where such inputs are processed and stored, and also whether they are themselves used as additional data to train generative AI configuration models.

Personal Data and Privacy Issues

It is worth mentioning that generative AI systems create significant problems in relation to the use and/or potential misuse of personal data, particularly in relation to GDPR compliance (although increasingly this is becoming a problem in US States that have implemented laws which attempt to create similar rights for data subjects, such as the CCPA in California).

In Chapter Six I address the interface between AI and data compliance in detail, which will generally be relevant to generative AI systems. This particular discussion deals with those data related issues that are specific to generative AI systems.

As with the intellectual property issues we have just considered, it is the massive web-scraping process used to train configuration models for generative AI which is causing concern for regulators. In particular, if information is being scraped on the scale we have discussed for these tools (in the magnitude of terabytes of data), how can the providers of these systems ensure that they have complied with their data related obligations?

To recap, the General Data Protection Regulation only allows for the processing of personal data if there is a lawful basis for processing of such data. As I discuss in Chapter Six in more detail, generally speaking this will only be permissible if there is a legitimate interest in such processing or the user has directly consented to such processing.

Legitimate interest is not available as a lawful basis in circumstances where there is automated decision making or profiling under Article 22 of the GDPR[34]. This means that direct consent needs to be used instead. In many US states, consent is also a pre-requisite to use of personal data.

This has created real difficulties for businesses such as OpenAI, particularly when attempting to release ChatGPT into Europe, and I would suggest is likely to become even more of a persistent issue across the European continent (including the UK, which, post-Brexit operates an essentially parallel GDPR data regime).

---

34 Automated processing is defined as a decision made by machine without meaningful human involvement which has legal effects or similarly significantly affects the data subject. Profiling includes the use of personal data to evaluate the characteristics of a natural person. See Chapter Six

On 12th April 2023, Italy's Data Protection regulator, the Garante[35] announced a temporary suspension of the service in Italy. In order to have the suspension lifted, OpenAI had to comply with a number of stipulations relating to its processing of personal data by 30th April 2023[36].

As at 30th April 2023, the ChatGPT service has been restored in Italy following steps taken by OpenAI to meet the compliance requirements set by the Garante. This will be without prejudice to additional investigations carried out by the Garante and an ad hoc task force set up by the European Data Protection Board[37].

Again, the extent to which generative AI services are likely to cause data compliance issues is, at the time of writing, a matter for active consideration by relevant regulators.

As with the intellectual property issues discussed earlier, the duty of practitioners is to determine the extent to which prevailing data protection regulatory standards have been complied with by the applicable provider and secure appropriate guarantees in licensing terms governing the provision of the relevant tool. If neither of these are attainable, then use of the relevant generative AI system will require a sensible risk benefit analysis, given the entire context of the immediate use case.

Additionally the same considerations in relation to user inputs into generative AI systems apply in relation to data protection, privacy and confidentiality – simply typing such information into a generative AI

35 The full title of Italy's regulator is *Garante per la protezione dei dati personali*

36 The full list of requirements is set out on the website of the Garante at https://www.garanteprivacy.it/web/guest/home/docweb/-/docweb-display/docweb/9874751#english

37 See https://edpb.europa.eu/news/news/2023/edpb-resolves-dispute-transfers-meta-and-creates-task-force-chat-gpt_en

system may breach confidentiality if the information is a trade secret or imparted in confidence; or in a regulated professional context (such as in the legal, medical or accountancy industries), may constitute a breach of applicable regulatory standards if it relates to a confidential client matter.

Generative AI Output Issues

As we have seen in Chapter One, Generative AI depends on machine learning which itself is an opaque "black box" technology. The models that are used by these systems depend heavily on forms of statistical probabilities to create their generative outputs. They are also trained on huge amounts of potentially unfiltered internet content. The biggest mistake uninitiated users can make is to assume (certainly insofar as the text generative models are concerned) that they are expert systems. They are not. Due to the nature of their architectures (and the current state of the art), they are incapable of verifying and referencing their outputs.

In fact, given the nature of the machine learning models that they use, it is well known that their outputs can be highly inaccurate or even invented[38]. Outputs may also be prone to bias or toxicity depending on the nature of training data used. This is not a new issue – back in 2016 a chat bot ("Tay") launched by Microsoft on Twitter and due to the nature of the training data presented by that environment, became a racist, homophobic Nazi. Unsurprisingly Microsoft pulled the plug on Tay after less than 24 hours online[39].

Licensing and liability issues

The next issue specific to generative AI relates to the manner in which it

---

38 There are multiple documented instances of these inventions (referred to as "*hallucinations*" by OpenAI's CEO, Sam Altman). Take for example the case of Steven Schwartz of Levidow, Levidow & Oberman who was sanctioned by the US District Court in June 2023 for using ChatGPT to draft a brief in a personal injury case. The brief cited several non-existent court cases

39 See https://www.gadgets360.com/social-networking/news/microsoft-pulls-the-plug-on-its-ai-chatbot-because-twitter-users-turned-it-into-a-giant-troll-817732

is accessed. As I mentioned at the beginning of this chapter, in addition to API access, most generative AI systems distinguish themselves from more conventional AI systems by being available through a "free" open access website, or one which requires a nominal subscription.

Of course "free" or "nominal" subscription in this sense means that you have traded access rights for no (or at least very limited) recourse against the relevant AI provider and they will have protected themselves with very restricted and limited liability levels. This means that in relation to the substantive issues we discussed relating to intellectual property, data protection and output quality, there will be no guarantees or effective contractual "guardrails" in place.

What steps can be taken to mitigate this? Again in practical terms it is often useful to understand that many of these generative AI tools are also available on an enterprise basis through established SaaS providers. So for example, Microsoft, which has a well-documented partnership with OpenAI, offers ChatGPT as part of its Azure product suite. In a similar vein, Google Cloud Services work with their own generative AI tool, Bard, and AWS (Amazon Web Services) have a partnership with Stability AI.

Employee Access Issues

Making such systems easily accessible via the public access websites we have just discussed presents additional problems for owners and operators of corporate IT systems that may have thousands of users.

In particular, the risks we considered earlier in relation to intellectual property, personal data and confidentiality can be magnified in an enterprise context and expose businesses to unacceptable levels of risk (and potential liability) if such generative AI systems are used indiscriminately by employees and other agents of the business. This is especially the case of course where the business in question is separately regulated and is bound by specific codes of conduct.

The clear analogy here is to indiscriminate use of the internet: generally it is established practice that businesses prohibit and/or block access to internet sites that promote pornography or violence or other harmful content, and put guidelines around acceptable use levels through the introduction of appropriate policies.

Although the risks presented by generative AI are somewhat different, businesses that are concerned about the risks involved in usage should be proactive and introduce similar measures in this context. In particular, one should be mindful not just of the corporate risks involved in using such systems but also of the employee-employer duty of care which may entail ensuring that employees are not exposed to content which may have a harmful effect on their well-being (whether physical or mental)[40] .

[40] For a particularly sobering account of what consequences could potentially be, see "*Man Dies by Suicide After talking with AI Chatbot*", Vice.com March 2023 https://www.vice.com/en/article/pkadgm/man-dies-by-suicide-after-talking-with-ai-chatbot-widow-says

CHAPTER FOUR

CAUSATION AND ARTIFICIAL INTELLIGENCE

AI Liability: A Sliding Scale

Liability is essentially a scalable concept which is based factually on the degree of legal responsibility society places on a ***person***. As we will see later on, historically responsibility and hence liability levels are not static – the able-minded, children and mentally incapable adults all have different levels of liability – the latter having little or no responsibility for their actions and therefore a commensurately lower level of accountability and liability.

The degree to which an artificially intelligent system could in theory assume responsibility for its actions thus depends, from a philosophical perspective (and taking aside any need to amend the law to account for such liability), on the extent to which it is aware of those actions. In the previous chapters, we have seen that the current state of the art is providing us with some very clever discrete (or narrow) solutions to particular problems and the advent of generative AI systems takes this level of machine competence even further. This does not yet equate however to human levels of sentience or even self-awareness.

Until relatively recently, the question of whether or not a machine should be accountable and hence liable for its actions was a relatively trite one – a machine was merely a tool of the person using or operating it. There was absolutely no question of machines assuming a level of personal accountability or even "*personhood*" as they were incapable of autonomous or semi-autonomous action. This is essentially the way in which the law has evolved to deal with machine generated consequences.

We are now however poised to deal with how to creatively twist our liability frameworks so as to account for the consequences created by autonomous machine action. Before we get into a discussion of existing liability frameworks, it is worth exploring this sliding scale theme. With this in mind, future liability frameworks are going to need to differentiate between traditional "dumb" machines at the one end, and super-intelligent semi or fully sentient machines at the other end.

A "*HAL 9000*" sentient supercomputer will have a greater degree of autonomy, independent thought and hence greater consequences coming from its action, and when it is created is very likely to be imbued with some form of personhood. In a sense, the two ends of the spectrum are easy to rationalise – the real conundrum is dealing with the liability consequences of a machine sandwiched between the HAL 9000 and the toaster: one which has properties of independent and autonomous action but not the clear attributes of a person as we understand it.

Complexity – A causative blocker

Taking aside the degree to which an AI system can assume awareness for its actions, there is a rather more immediate problem in the usage of current AI systems which is driven by the legal concept of ***causation***. We will look at existing liability frameworks shortly, but put simply, in order to establish liability you need to demonstrate that the person or thing *caused* the relevant loss or damage.

Existing causative liability models work well when machine functions (and hence responses) can by and large be traced back to human design, programming and knowledge.

In machine learning systems this is usually very difficult to achieve especially in artificial neural networks or probabilistic Bayesian networks where computer scientists are often unable to determine how or why (on a human explicable basis) a machine learning system has made a particular decision.

The current "*state of the art*" does not provide for systems to self-report their decisions, but there is a widely held view in the relevant scientific community that regulators will ultimately force developers to interject "explanation systems" into their AI solutions where they are deployed in environments where their outputs (or decisions) are likely to have a significant regulatory or human impact such as healthcare or financial services.

There are technical concerns however that these explanation systems may impair or limit the operation of the core machine learning system (by constraining them to a narrower spectrum of decisions that are human explicable) and may be of limited use where the rationale or decision adopted by the ML system is not capable of human explanation. As noted earlier, probabilistic Bayesian networks and artificial neural networks are particularly difficult to decipher owing to their structures – decision trees may be slightly easier (decision tree networks that are organised into Random Forests may however regain "*black box*" characteristics).

Interestingly, there is a current theoretical view that distributive, decentralised blockchain technology may provide the ideal characteristics for an auditable framework for such explanation systems by underpinning and logging in an immutable way each step of the artificial reasoning process – however we are some distance from any such auditing technology being introduced in practical terms.

Aside from the question of whether a decision is traceable from a causative viewpoint, it may also be incorrect to classify an undesired decision or "*learned behaviour*" adopted by a machine learning system as subjectively wrong – just because a system produces an undesirable result does not mean it is defective.

As I mentioned in Chapter Two, AI systems are renowned for what are known as their "*edge case*" decisions – those decisions which are at the margins of the probability curve for their operating parameters. Much scientific effort is devoted to tuning out these edge cases, but they still occur (indeed in some cases these outcomes may be positively encouraged).

Counterfactual Analysis

Finally, on the issue of explicability and machine learning, it is worth briefly mentioning the concept of counterfactuals as a mathematical response. What a counterfactual aims to do is essentially provide a rationale for a given circumstance by positing what might have happened had the given circumstance *not* actually occurred – for example *had I not stepped onto the ice, I wouldn't have slipped.*

In machine learning, counterfactual analysis can be used to explain how a machine learning model got to a particular prediction, which is a particularly useful technique given the opaque nature of many of these systems.

In machine learning, the prediction itself is the outcome, and the particular parameters or "*feature values*" which were input into the model are the causes of that outcome. Changing these feature values cause the prediction to change but not necessarily in a way which reflects the real causal relationships of the data in the machine learning model. Hence you can arrive at a plausible "cause" without actually understanding the real reason the model predicted in the way that it did. Of course, whilst valuable, counterfactuals can introduce an additional problem of multiple truths – or the so-called Rashomon effect[41], itself mitigated by evaluating all counterfactual explanations in any given instance and prioritising them for suitability and likelihood.

Existing liability frameworks

So, with this in mind, let's review the existing liability frameworks which could conceivably apply to what are termed "*machine generated*

41 This was named after the Japanese movie "Rashomon" which features the murder of a Samurai and the multiple, contradicting but highly plausible explanations for his murder provided by several witnesses

consequences". Current liability frameworks are focussed on product liability generally – broken down into three distinct categories: Contract law, Negligence (tort) and, so far as the UK (and EU) is concerned, strict liability under consumer protection legislation (in the UK the Consumer Protection Act 1987).

We'll review the scope of each briefly in a moment and then consider potential issues in relation to their application to AI systems. In this context, the most conventional analysis we can apply to intelligent or semi-intelligent machines is as complex products.

Using the driverless car as an example, what we can see is that in fact it is an assemblage of many and varied integrated systems that are produced by multiple manufacturers. For a driverless car to work effectively, it needs sensors to navigate road obstructions, such as radar and lidar detection. It must have a computer to direct its actions and that computer needs to have a logic framework within which to operate – internally by use of its own operating software and also externally by reference to map data. All of these systems need to work together effectively, and this is without consideration of all the usual mechanical components which form a standard car, which must also be present and functioning.

Taking aside the organisational complexity of the AI system itself which we have already discussed, this mechanical complexity alone gives rise to a potential plethora of liability targets, ranging from the vehicle manufacturer itself, all the way down to the designer of an individual component, depending upon where the actual defect, fault or breach occurs.

Contract

Contract clearly has a role to play in determining product-based liability. Contracts ensure that manufacturers and retailers sell products that meet agreed pre-determined standards. Such liability is obviously aimed at the recovery of financial (or pure economic) loss as a result of breach of these contractual standards, however obviously, as we are all aware, contract liability can in some circumstances lead to the recovery of damages for consequential loss.

Contract terms and hence liability may be either express – as to defects and warranties or implied. In the UK there are implied terms as to quality, fitness for purpose, title and description in the Consumer Rights Act 2015 so far as B2C contracts are concerned and the Sale of Goods Act 1979 for B2B contracts. Although there is not a focus on "*defects*" per se under the Sale of Goods legislation, there is clearly an emphasis on conformity with description. Arguably that could amount to nearly the same thing: a failure to conform to a description or specification is very close to a "*defect*" in practical terms.

We'll take a look at the relevant strengths and weaknesses of contract liability in this context in a moment, but it is worth remembering that contract is a ***causative*** based liability framework. In order to found liability, the Claimant must prove that there was a breach of either an express or an implied term and that that breach caused the loss. Contract causation is often overlooked as the poor cousin of tort causation but ever since the time of ***Hadley v. Baxendale***[42], it is still a relevant factor in determining liability. This is an important consideration – and again one we'll return to later.

Finally, it is worth remembering that the primary remedy for breach of contract is damages (as assessed to put the innocent party in the position they would have been had the contract been correctly performed). The primary advantage of contract liability is of course that it is open to the contract counterparties to determine the scope of the contract responsibilities and obligations as between them and hence the liability if things do go wrong. This means that it is quite open to tailor the agreement to the functions and performance of the AI system involved.

So far as the implied terms are concerned, Section 9 of the Consumer Rights Act provides that where goods are sold "in the course of a

42 [1854] EWHC J70

business" there is an implied term that the goods are of *satisfactory quality*[43] and *fit for a purpose*[44] that the buyer has made known to the seller. Products are therefore of satisfactory quality if they meet the standard that a reasonable person would regard as satisfactory, taking into account their description, price and all other relevant circumstances. In other words it could be argued that contract implied terms create a consumer expectation test.

The major disadvantage of contract liability of course is that it is not a liability that applies generally to the "whole world" but rather is one which is constrained by *contract privity* (albeit with limited exceptions in some jurisdictions – such as the Contract (Rights of Third Parties) Act 1999 in the UK).

This means that obligations can only be enforced by contract counterparties. Of course – in some situations it is possible to conceive of a contract relationship subsisting in your use of an intelligent systems – but equally speaking in many others, there will not be. Aside from this, there is a lack of consistency in contractual standards in relation to contracts for the sale of goods which make the application of the framework complex. So, for example, for public policy reasons there are higher standards which apply to contracts made with consumers – the Consumer Rights Act requires that in assessing whether products are of satisfactory quality that account is taken of any "*public statements on the specific characteristics of the goods made about them by the Seller or the producer, particularly in advertising*"[45].

Tort

Product liability in tort refers to a breach of a duty of care in negligence.

---

[43] s9

[44] s10

[45] s9(5)

Since the seminal case of *Donoghue v. Stevenson*[46], tortious duties can run concurrently with contractual liabilities. The essence of the case was that if a consumer purchases products in a form intended to reach him or her without the possibility of reasonable intermediate examination and with the knowledge on the part of the producer that the absence of reasonable care in the preparation of the product will result in personal injury or property damage, which is reasonably foreseeable, then that producer owes a duty to take reasonable care in their production. *Donoghue v. Stevenson* concerned decomposed snails in ginger beer bottles but it does not take much to extrapolate that analysis to a driverless car or a surgical robot.

Again, it is worth pointing out the causative nature of tort as a liability framework – it is essentially fault based. The claimant must prove that the defendant owed him or her a duty of care, they failed in that standard and damage was caused as a result.

In contrast to contractual damages, tort-based damages are awarded on the basis of putting the injured party in the position they would have been had the tort not occurred. The scope of potential liability in tort is wide. It could equally apply to manufacturers, producers and anyone directly involved in the manufacture and distribution of a product with a defect. You do however need to establish that a duty of care subsists and was breached – and irrespective of this that the relevant chain of causation is not broken by the damage being too remote.

There are a number of disadvantages with this liability framework – and it is worth pointing them out briefly. There are very real difficulties in claiming damages for pure economic loss in tort – certainly so far as the UK is concerned, and since the high watermark of *Junior Books v. Veitchi*[47], there are only a limited number of circumstances where this is

---

46 [1932] AC 562

47 [1983] 1 AC 520

possible, including for example, negligent advice from surveyors.

Contributory negligence can also act as a defence to liability, if it is shown that the claimant should have known of the defect but negligently failed to recognise it or negligently used the product or failed to take account of its operating instructions. In such cases damages are reduced to a degree which is commensurate with the claimant's negligence.

Volenti non fit injuria – or voluntary assumption of risk is less common in product liability cases – on the basis that if a claimant knows of the defect they are less likely to use it and if they do, that usually breaks the causative chain between defect and damage.

As we have seen, as intelligent machines and AI systems "learn" for themselves, their behaviours are increasingly less and less directly attributable to human programming. These machines are not acting on a prescriptive instruction set, but a system of rules that may not have anticipated the precise circumstances under which the machine should act. To take our prior example of the autonomous vehicle, what if our car has been programmed to look after and preserve the safety of its occupants and also to avoid pedestrians at all costs and is placed in an unavoidable situation where it has to make a decision as to whether to avoid a pedestrian crossing into its path (and thereby run into a brick wall, injuring or even killing its occupants) or running over the pedestrian (and thereby saving its occupants). Can any outcome of that decision be said to be a failure or a defect – even if people are injured or possibly killed as a result?[48]

In tort, the doctrine of *res ipsa loquitur* – or the thing speaks for itself assists in providing a partial solution to the problem. The doctrine is equally applicable in the US and the UK.

---

48 This is the so-called "trolley car" problem postulated by Philippa Foot in "*The Problem of Abortion and the Doctrine of the Double Effect*" Oxford Review, Number 5, 1967

Res ipsa loquitur is useful in dealing with cases where there are multiple successive inexplicable failures which cannot in themselves be readily explained. A classic example of the application of this was in the US case of *Toyota Motor Corporation*[49], where Toyota found that for no particular reason, many of its high-end Lexus model cars simply accelerated – despite the intervention of their drivers. After extensive investigation, the cause of these failures could not be pinpointed by the manufacturer. Toyota took the step of settling 400 pending cases against it after a jury applied the doctrine *of res ipsa loquitur* and awarded the plaintiffs in that case $3m in damages.

In the UK the principles are enshrined in the leading case of *Scott and Bennett v Chemical Construction (GB) Ltd*[50]. This provides for a three-step test for the principle to be applied: (i) the event or accident would not ordinarily have occurred in the absence of negligence (ii) the thing causing the damage must be under the control of the defendant and (iii) there is no evidence as to the cause of the event or accident. Clearly such a test will need to be considered in the context of artificially intelligent machines and the extent to which such a device can be considered to be "under the control" of its user when it is making decisions on its own behalf will be debateable to a greater or lesser degree. What this doctrine also does not provide a solution to of course is the inexplicable *isolated* incident.

Finally, it should be emphasised that on a factual basis, proving liability in tort can be very difficult – especially in product liability cases, as very often the details that are required to show liability are held by the defendant. Obviously there are mechanisms in litigation to get hold of that information – but typically a defendant will not go out of the way to disclose it and might use any number of established disclosure tricks

---

49 See *In re Toyota Motor Corp. unintended acceleration marketing, sales practices and products liability litigation*, 978 F.Supp.2d 1053 (C.D.Cal. 2013), 92 Fed. R. Evid. Serv. 714, Prod.Liab.Rep. (CCH) P 19, 244, 2013 WL 5763178

50 [1971] 3 All ER 822

to bury the key facts or at least make them very difficult to ascertain.

The draft EU AI Liability Directive

As we shall see in Chapter Five, these evidential difficulties, particularly in machine learning cases, have been recognised by EU authorities as potentially impeding access to justice by EU Citizens. As a response to this (and in fact an acknowledgement that the EU Artificial Intelligence Act contains no substantive private rights of action), the EU AI Liability Directive proposes (amongst other measures) a rebuttable presumption of causality[51] which places the burden of proof on AI providers rather than users[52].

Strict Liability: Consumer Protection

The Consumer Protection Act 1987 ("CPA") implements the EU directive on Liability for Defective Products[53]. This Act introduces a strict liability regime which does not affect the general availability of Contract and Tort based remedies. What the Act provides is that a person who is injured or whose personal property is damaged by a product will be able to claim against a manufacturer or supplier of that product (and certain other third parties) if it can be shown that the product was defective.

There is no requirement to prove fault on the part of the manufacturer but obviously there is a requirement on the claimant to show that the defect existed on the preponderance of the evidence. The Act introduces a consumer expectations test in that a defect exists where "*the safety of the product is not such as persons generally are entitled to expect*"[54]. Consumer expectations themselves are subject to a reasonableness test.

---

[51] See Article 4 of the AI Liability Directive

[52] See discussion in Chapter Five

[53] 85/374/EC

[54] s3(1)

In terms of the advantages of the CPA regime – as previously discussed – there is no requirement to show fault; neither is there a privity requirement – the regime itself allows for a wide variety of potential liability targets, including suppliers and manufacturers.

There are still some problems with consumer protection product liability however – obviously causation still exists – although it is limited to the finding of defects and moderated by a consumer expectation test. Furthermore, the Act is designed to cover claims for real damage, so does not encompass claims for pure economic loss.

In the context of artificial intelligence, we are now at a clear inflexion point and post-Brexit divergence as between product liability treatment under the laws of the UK and the EU. As we'll see in Chapter Five, the proposed EU draft Artificial Intelligence Act now explicitly brings some classes of AI system into the EU product liability regime. As the UK does not have any plans to adopt the AIA, the prior position established under the UK CPA regime remains. So far as AI systems are concerned, there are clear problems with the definition of "*Product*" under the UK Act. Product is defined as "*any goods or electricity and includes products aggregated into other products, whether as component parts, raw materials or otherwise*"[55]. Quite ambiguously for our purposes the Act is not clear as to whether software and/or other products of an intellectual type are included in the definition of its scope. Disembodied software per se is typically not treated as a "good" under English law although there is an argument which might encompass software embedded into functional hardware. Anecdotally, the Consumer Rights Act may also provide some correlative instruction so far as Sale of Goods legislation is concerned in its Chapter 3, which explicitly provides that the supply of digital content should be treated neither as goods nor as a service but as a separate class of supply[56].

---

[55] s1(2)(c)

[56] s33 et seq

Finally, there is also the "*developmental risks defence*", which provides a defence to the manufacturer "*if the scientific and technical knowledge at the time the product was manufactured was not such that a producer of a similar product might have been able to discover the defect*"[57]. This is obviously highly relevant to our current discussion – products including machine learning and artificial intelligence will inevitably involve the "state of the art" in relation to their development.

Insurance

Insurance clearly has a role to play in this context as well, particularly in the context of autonomous vehicles.

These so called CAVs[58] create particular causation issues which have the potential to disrupt the way in which road traffic accidents are handled from a claims perspective. The key concern being that if a car is involved in an accident when it is "self-piloting" who should be liable? The vehicle manufacturer or the driver?

In response to this issue, the UK Government recently enacted the Automated and Electric Vehicles Act 2018 (the AEVA 2018).

Section 2(1) of the AEVA 2018 provides that "*where...an accident is caused by an automated vehicle when driving itself...the vehicle is insured at the time of the accident, and...an insured person or any other person suffers damage as a result of the accident, the insurer is liable for that damage.*"

In essence the principle enshrined in the Act is that if you are hit by an insured party's vehicle that is self-driving at the time, the insurer "at fault" pays out. If you have comprehensive cover then you will also be insured for your own injuries. If the vehicle at fault is not covered by insurance then the Motor Insurers Bureau will pay out in the usual way and seek to

[57] s4(1)e

[58] Connected and autonomous vehicles

recover its losses from the owner of the uninsured vehicle.

This is an essentially pragmatic response that will probably work in an environment where there is a mixed demographic of driverless cars and human piloted ones – it also avoids systemic change to the insurance industry.

Crucially, the measure relies very heavily on the ability of insurers to subrogate and therefore bring claims of their own against other third parties, including manufacturers. This will of course be hugely problematic for insurers if the relevant fault or defect cannot easily be traced.

Individuation or Artificial Personhood

The last topic in this chapter that we touch upon is a brief discussion of *artificial personhood* as this is a liability concept that has ignited much debate.

We have already hopefully dispelled the myth that AGI or artificial general intelligence is a close prospect. It is however worth considering briefly the inevitable question of how our liability rules will cope with machines if at some stage they do *individuate* – or develop distinct legal personalities and individual identities of their own. Clearly if machines possess a human equivalent personality of their own then there is no reason why they cannot directly accrue liability through the concept of "*artificial personhood*" in the same manner in which living breathing humans accrue it. The European Parliament considered this question in a recommendation on granting robots and AI's legal status to the Commission on *Civil Law Rules on Robotics*[59]. Part of their recommended approach was to propose a registration system for intelligent robots. The recommendation on special legal personality was ultimately criticised in an open letter to the Commission signed by over 150 AI and robotics

---

[59] 27th January 2017 2015/2103 (INL), see in particular paragraph 59 f

specialists.

For the more distant future, there are no answers here obviously, but rather questions. We can however consider some current and historical legal analogues. How are we going to treat self-aware machines and are we going to fall into the unfortunate historical bear traps of the past? The historical treatment of slaves bears particular scrutiny in this regard and the questions raised by that treatment are no less relevant now, although not for discussion in this book.

If we walk further down the path of individuation, and give them personal liability, how are we going to apply legal duties of care to intelligent machines?

Obviously the law already recognises circumstances where there is a reduced level of legal liability owing to a commensurately reduced ability to distinguish right from wrong – the principle of *Doli Incapax* in relation to infants and the mentally incapable spring to mind in this regard. Might some machines that are not fully capable of understanding the consequences of their actions fall within this principle in the future?

We are now effectively at a "*tipping point*" in how we manage the machine generated consequences of our new AI creations. As we have seen, Contract, Tort and Strict Liability consumer protection laws are effective to a degree in relation to managing these consequences but effectively break down where cause and effect cannot be made out.

In the next chapter we examine how the European Union has proposed rising to these challenges and in particular how the new draft EU Artificial Intelligence Act and Draft Liability Directive will ultimately regulate AI systems.

CHAPTER FIVE

THE EU ARTIFICIAL INTELLIGENCE ACT

Introduction

Since the last publication of this book, the European Union's grand vision for an AI regulatory regime, as expressed by the President of the European Commission, Ursula Von Der Leyen[60] has moved closer to finalisation. Although the EU Artificial Intelligence Act (the "EU AIA") is still currently in draft form (alongside it's companion measure, the AI Liability Directive) it is now sufficiently advanced to form the basis of a discussion in this edition, particularly as it seems likely that the law itself is likely to become as globally influential as the GDPR was for data-related regimes.

Companies that intend to market AI Systems for use by EU consumers within the European Union, whether or not they are domiciled in the Union should have regard to its provisions. As such, in a global digital economy, it seems likely that the measure will have a significant extra-territorial impact.

A word of warning however that there are however a number of legislative hurdles which will need to be passed before the measure actually becomes law within the EU and as such any commentary made in this edition is inevitably going to be superseded by the time the regulation is finally adopted.

---

60 On 19 February 2020, the Commission President introduced a digital strategy for Europe. See *White Paper on Artificial Intelligence: a European approach to excellence and trust*: https://commission.europa.eu/publications/white-paper-artificial-intelligence-european-approach-excellence-and-trust_en

In the meantime, it is worthwhile outlining what progress has actually been made legislatively, as this is characterised somewhat by the complicated trilateral nature of the EU governance model, and the need to ensure that all EU institutions (the Commission, the Council and the Parliament) have commented upon and approved the proposed law.

Generally speaking, progression on the measure was significantly delayed, initially by the onset of the Covid-19 Pandemic, and subsequently by concerns raised by EU parliamentarians on the risks posed to society by the use of Generative AI systems[61] (or "*Foundational AI Models*" that have been specialised for generative content as they are referred to in various iterations of the EU AIA).

On 21st April, 2021, the European Commission proposed an initial original draft of the EU AIA[62]. This I refer to as the Commission AIA Proposal[63].

On 15th July 2022, the Czech Presidency of the EU Council presented a final Council Compromise Version of the AIA, incorporating amendments recommended by the EU 27 member states. I refer to this as the Council Compromise Text[64].

Finally, on 14th June 2023, the EU Parliament finalised its amendments

---

61 See Chapter Three on Generative AI Systems for a more detailed discussion of these types of AI systems

62 ***Proposal for a REGULATION OF THE EUROPEAN PARLIAMENT AND OF THE COUNCIL LAYING DOWN HARMONISED RULES ON ARTIFICIAL INTELLIGENCE (ARTIFICIAL INTELLIGENCE ACT) AND AMENDING CERTAIN UNION LEGISLATIVE ACTS,*** *COM/2021/206 final,* see: https://eur-lex.europa.eu/legal-content/EN/TXT/?qid=1623335154975&uri=CELEX:52021PC0206

63 For a detailed commentary and analysis of the Commission AIA Proposal, please see ITechLaw's Green Paper: *The EU AIA, A Green Paper Policy Analysis* available for download at https://www.itechlaw.org/eu-aia-green-paper

64 See https://artificialintelligenceact.eu/wp-content/uploads/2022/07/AIA-CZ-1st-Proposal-15-July.pdf

for the EU AIA. I refer to this as the EU Parliament Text[65]. Much of the commentary that follows in this chapter is based on this latest proposal.

As at the date of writing, the Commission, Council and Parliament have now entered what is referred to as a "trilogue" negotiation phase to reach political agreement on a final adopted version of the EU AIA. Typically such discussions last three to four months. However, given the significance of this measure and the wide-ranging (potentially controversial) nature of some of the amendments proposed in the Amended Parliament Text, it is not expected to become law before the first quarter of 2024, at the earliest.

Artificial Intelligence Definitions

Before we delve into a discussion of the structure of the EU AIA, it is worth spending some time examining how it treats the definition of "*Artificial Intelligence*". This is highly significant as most of the compliance obligations in the act will spring from a consideration of whether the system in question actually falls within the definition. There were some criticisms of the breadth of the core definition in the Commission AIA Proposal, which have subsequently been adjusted by the Council Compromise Text and the Amended Parliament Text.

Annex I of the Commission AIA Proposal[66] referred not only to Machine Learning approaches[67], but also to "*Logic and knowledge-based approaches, including...inductive (logic) programming, knowledge bases...*"[68] and "*Statistical approaches...search and optimization methods*"[69], neither of which purists would argue, were machine learning or artificial

65 EU Parliament reference P9 TA(2023)0236 https://www.europarl.europa.eu/doceo/document/TA-9-2023-0236_EN.pdf

66 Annexes, see Note 3 above

67 See Annex I, para (a)

68 Annex I, para (b)

69 Annex I, para (c)

intelligence. In fact some have argued that the latter two paragraphs could encompass (in the broadest sense) technologies such as search engines and macro enabled spreadsheets.

This criticism was fully recognized in the subsequent Council Compromise texts and EU Parliament Texts which have discarded the above in favour of a more AI aligned and technology neutral definition (the following is the Amendment proposed in the adopted EU Parliament Text):

> *"'artificial intelligence system' (AI system) means a machine-based system that is designed to operate with varying levels of autonomy and that can, for explicit or implicit objectives, generate outputs such as predictions, recommendations, or decisions, that influence physical or virtual environments;"*[70]

Foundation Models

One of the technological issues not captured in the original Commission AIA Proposal, or indeed the Council Compromise Text, is the concept of the "*foundation model*" (as it is referred to in the EU Parliament Text). Foundation models are, in essence, general purpose AI systems. Such models become "generative AI systems" when trained to generate AI content, such as images and text. This concept represents a radical change to the structure of the EU AIA and is, in policy terms, intended to capture these latest generative AI systems[71]. In effect the EU Parliament Text introduces a parallel 'bolt-on' compliance regime for these models. it defines these as follows:

---

70 See Amendment 165 of the EU Parliament Text

71 See Chapter Three. The Council Compromise text introduced the concept of "General Purpose AI" which was originally framed as a general exemption to compliance requirements, now deleted due to its potential conflict with the increased use of (and concerns surrounding) generative AI Systems. Somewhat confusingly (as it partially overlaps with the "foundation model" definition) the concept is retained in the EU Parliament Text

> *"…'foundation model' means an AI system model that is trained on broad data at scale, is designed for generality of output, and can be adapted to a wide range of distinctive tasks"*[72]

The explanation in Recital 60g of the EU Parliament Text provides some explanation for the approach adopted:

> *"There is significant uncertainty as to the way foundation models will evolve, both in terms of typology of models and in terms of self-governance. Therefore, it is essential to clarify the legal situation of providers of foundation models… These specific requirements and obligations do not amount to considering foundation models as high risk AI systems, but should guarantee that the objectives of this Regulation … are achieved."*[73]

The core compliance requirements for foundation models are set out in a new Article 28 b[74]. The providers of such models must comply with these requirements prior to making them available on the market or putting them into service, regardless of whether they are providing the system as a standalone model or embedded in a wider product and irrespective of whether it us offered under free or open-source licenses[75]:

Risk Mitigation and Reduction[76]

Providers need to demonstrate through appropriate design testing and analysis that they have identified and addressed (and taken steps to reduce) all reasonably forseeable risks to health, safety, fundamental

---

72 See Amendment 168 of the EU Parliament Text (note 9 above for document reference)

73 See Amendment 102 of the EU Parliament Text (note 9 above for document reference)

74 See Amendment 399 of the EU Parliament Text (note 9 above for document reference)

75 Article 28 b 1 (amendment 399)

76 Article 28 b 2 (a)

rights, the environment, democracy and the rule of law, prior to and throughout development of the foundation model. Providers should use appropriate methods to do this, including the involvement of independent experts and documenting remaining non-mitigable risks after development.

Dataset Hygiene[77]

Datasets for foundation models must be subject to "appropriate" data governance measures, in particular measures to assess the suitability of the data sources used for foundation purposes and also to examine possible biases and mitigation.

Performance Standards[78]

The design and development of a foundation model should achieve (throughout its lifecycle) appropriate levels of "*performance, predictability, interpretability, corrigibility, safety and cybersecurity*" to be assessed by means such as model evaluation using independent experts, documented analysis and extensive testing.

Environmental Impacts[79]

Foundation models should make use of applicable standards to reduce energy use, resources and waste as well as increase energy efficiency. They should also be designed with capabilities to measure the consumption of energy and resources over their entire lifecycle.

Technical Documentation[80]

Providers should draw up extensive technical documentation and

77 Article 28 b 2 (b)

78 Article 28 b 2 (c)

79 Article 28 b 2 (d)

80 Article 28 b 2 (e)

intelligible instructions for the use of foundation models, to enable downstream providers to comply with their own regulatory obligations.

Quality Management System[81]

Quality management systems need to be established to ensure compliance with these requirements.

Registration in EU-wide Database[82]

Providers and, depending upon relevant circumstances, deployers of AI systems, must ensure that the foundation model is registered in the EU database referred to in Article 60[83].

Providers of Foundational AI systems which are specifically intended to be used as generative AI systems (creating complex text, image, audio and/or video outputs) are also required to comply with the transparency provisions of the AIA (requiring disclosure that the content was AI generated[84]) provide adequate safeguards to ensure that such content is not generated in breach of applicable EU law[85], and to publish a sufficiently detailed summary of training data used that is protected under copyright law.

At the time of writing it is of course unclear whether the approach adopted by the EU Parliament will survive the trilogue negotiations which are currently being undertaken by the EU institutions (or whether indeed this concept will be absorbed into the more established "high risk" category of AI system we discuss below). These standards, whilst

---

81 Article 28 b 2 (f)

82 Article 28 b 2 (g)

83 Article 60 introduces a new requirement to register systems on an EU wide database. See later on in this chapter

84 See Article 52 (amendment 484) et seq of the EU Parliament Text

85 Applicable laws in this context would presumably include laws relating to intellectual property, and principally breach of copyright.

admirable, are still ambiguous in scope in relation to the actual levels of detailed compliance which will be required. This is partly due to the entirely novel nature of foundation models and is a point acknowledged directly by the EU Parliament in the associated recitals to the new Article[86].

General Principles for AI

The EU AIA creates a regulatory model which is very heavily linked to the existing European product safety regime.

Rather than adopting an "*outcomes based*" approach[87] the Commission AIA Proposal was largely based on defined classes of use case. Conceptually this is a very elegant way to insert the measure into the existing EU product safety framework but, as the introduction of generative AI has subsequently demonstrated to European legislators, it makes it harder to adapt the law for changes in what is a rapidly advancing technology.

In an attempt to moderate this approach, one of the changes the EU Parliament Text introduces is the concept of general underlying principles set out in Article 4 a[88]. This Article is intended to be applied to all AI systems (regardless of risk classification) as well as Foundation models. As you will see, there is a very high degree of alignment to core

86 See recitals 60 e, 60 f, 60 g and 60 h respectively (amendments 99, 100, 101 and 102) of the EU Parliament Text

87 An outcomes-based approach looks at the impact of harms on the relevant subject. This is used in a data-based context by Article 22 of the GDPR on Automated Decision making and profiling which takes into account the impact of automated decisions on data subjects and only includes those within its definition which have a legal effect or similarly significantly affect data subjects. See Chapter Six for a more detailed discussion

88 See Amendment 213 of the EU Parliament Text (note 9 above for document reference)

AI ethical principles in their formulation[89].

The key general principles are as follows[90]:

- *Human agency and oversight*

  AI systems need to be developed and used as tools to serve people. They should respect human dignity and autonomy and ensure appropriate levels of human oversight and control.

- *Technical robustness and safety*

  AI systems need to be developed in a way to minimise harm and should be robust in the case of unintended problems. They should also be resilient to malicious attempts to alter their performance.

- *Privacy and data governance*

  Such systems need to be developed and used consistent with existing privacy and data protection rules and process data that is high quality.

- *Transparency*

  AI systems should be developed and used in a way which allows for appropriate explainability and traceability as well as making it evident to human users that they are communicating with a machine. The capabilities of AI systems and their limitations need to be informed to users.

---

89 See Chapter Two

90 See Amendment 213 of the EU Parliament Text (note 9 above for document reference)

- *Diversity, non-discrimination and fairness*

  AI systems should be developed and used in a way which includes diverse actors and promotes equal access, gender equality and cultural diversity. They should also avoid discriminatory impacts and unfair biases.

- *Social and environmental well-being*

  Finally, AI Systems should be used in a sustainable and environmentally friendly manner, benefiting human society. Long term impacts on individuals, society and democracy should be monitored.

Prohibited AI, High Risk AI and Everything Else

Aside from the inclusion of foundation models in a parallel compliance regime which is part of a late addition to the new EU Parliament Text, the EU AIA provides for a three-tier regulatory regime.

It is a useful metaphor for the regime to be categorised as a pyramid – which was in fact how the EU commissioners explained it at the press conference launching the draft measure. At the very tip or apex of the pyramid are the proposed prohibited uses of AI (referred to as "Prohibited AI"), within the middle band sits "High Risk" AI – and finally the base comprises everything else. We'll look at each of these tiers shortly.

There are some overarching measures, such as transparency (and now the general principles for AI previously mentioned), which apply across all permitted systems.

In terms of other considerations to take note of, the measure is sector agnostic. This means that it will apply irrespective of (and in addition to) any sector-based regulation that may apply in relation to any particular AI use cases. It is also important to note that it has clearly been designed to complement the regulatory framework for data which has been created by the GDPR.

The AIA applies most of its compliance measures to what are termed "*AI Service Providers*" (although as we shall see subsequently, there are specific obligations for deployers, distributors and importers of such systems into the EU).

There has been some criticism directed at the framers of the originally drafted Commission AIA Proposal for taking what is essentially an enterprise view of AI system creation. "*AI Service Providers*" in this context are the creators of end-to-end AI systems. This definition works very well in a scenario where you are licensing a system from an established provider such as Microsoft Azure or AWS. It however becomes less clear what the term actually refers to when applied to the burgeoning open access MLOps machine learning markets hosted by GitHub and Linux Foundation[91].

The EU Parliament Text addresses this potential issue by stating that the regulation should not apply "*…to AI components provided under free and open-source licences except to the extent they are placed on the market or put into service by a provider as part of a high-risk AI system…*"[92]

Prohibited AI

When the Original Commission AIA Proposal was introduced in 2021, an attempt was made to define potential use cases for AI systems which would be considered unacceptable, taking into account the fundamental democratic standards of the European Union.

The EU Parliament Text has made some significant amendments to these provisions and has also expanded and clarified the context to which the

91 See Chapter Twelve

92 See Amendment 164 of the EU Parliament Text (note 9 above for document reference)

categories relate, with a much heavier focus on individual human rights. As the measure currently stands, Prohibited AI classes comprise[93]:

- *the placing on the market, putting into service or use of an AI system that deploys subliminal techniques beyond a person's consciousness or purposefully manipulative or deceptive techniques, with the objective to or the effect of materially distorting a person's or a group of persons' behaviour by appreciably impairing the person's ability to make an informed decision, thereby causing the person to take a decision that that person would not have otherwise taken in a manner that causes or is likely to cause that person, another person or group of persons significant harm*[94]*;*

- *the placing on the market, putting into service or use of an AI system that exploits any of the vulnerabilities of a person or a specific group of persons, including characteristics of such person's or a such group's known or predicted personality traits or social or economic situation age, physical or mental ability with the objective or to the effect of materially distorting the behaviour of that person or a person pertaining to that group in a manner that causes or is likely to cause that person or another person significant harm;*

- *the placing on the market, putting into service or use of biometric categorisation systems that categorise natural persons according to sensitive or protected attributes or characteristics or based on the inference of those attributes or characteristics;*[95]

93 Generally see Amendments 215 to 227 of the EU Parliament Text

94 There is an exception to this for systems that use subliminal techniques for therapeutic purposes with the informed consent of the relevant patient

95 Article 5 1 b a (Amendment 217 of the EU Parliament Text). This prohibition is again subject to a therapeutic use exception. It is interesting in that it would appear at first sight to create a tension with both the provisions of the GDPR

- *the placing on the market, putting into service or use of AI systems for the social scoring evaluation or classification of the trustworthiness of natural persons or groups thereof over a certain period of time based on their social behaviour or known, inferred or predicted personal or personality characteristics, with the social score leading to … detrimental or unfavourable treatment…;*

- *the use of 'real-time' biometric identification systems in publicly accessible spaces;*[96]

- *the placing on the market, putting into service or use of an AI system for making risk assessments of natural persons or groups …in order to assess the risk of a natural person for offending or reoffending or for predicting the occurrence or reoccurrence of an actual or potential criminal or administrative offence based on profiling of a natural person or on assessing personality traits and characteristics, including the person's location, or past criminal behaviour …;*

- *The placing on the market, putting into service or use of AI systems that create or expand facial recognition databases through the untargeted scraping of facial images from the internet or CCTV footage;*[97]

---

which relate to automated decision making and profiling using special category data – see Articles 22 and 9 of the GDPR, and the AIA's own 'High Risk' Biometric system category set out under Annex III (see later discussion in this chapter).

96 Article 5 1 c (Amendment 218 of the EU Parliament Text). This prohibition has been substantially widened in the European Parliament Text – previously this prohibition was limited to use by law enforcement authorities for the purposes of law enforcement. This will have very real and severe consequences for AFR (automated facial recognition) applications in the EU should it enter law – for a fuller discussion, see Chapter Seven

97 This prohibited use case is clearly designed to explicitly prevent the type of behaviour exhibited by Clearview AI, which has been censured by domestic and

- *the placing on the market, putting into service or use of AI systems to infer emotions of a natural person in the areas of law enforcement, border management, in workplace and education institutions;*

- *the putting into service or use of AI systems for the analysis of recorded footage of publicly accessible spaces through 'post' remote biometric identification systems, unless they are subject to a pre-judicial authorisation ... and strictly necessary for the targeted search connected to a specific serious criminal offense ... that already took place for the purpose of law enforcement.*

Aside from the first two classes of Prohibited AI, which remain largely unchanged from the Council Compromise Text (and which are designed to cover the most egregious examples of manipulative and distortive AI use), the new and expanded classes of Prohibited AI as framed in the EU Parliament Text, will, to the extent they are adopted, place significant constraints on the use of predictive policing techniques throughout the EU, including recording of surveillance footage for later analysis, emotion detection systems and in a non-law enforcement context, prohibit the use (by any entity) of automated facial recognition systems that are placed in publicly accessible spaces[98]. They also, as we will see, create some overlaps with the 'High Risk' categories which will require further guidance and clarification.

Finally, it is worth noting the exclusions – specifically that the regulation as drafted does not apply in military contexts[99]. It also does not apply in

---

international regulators for its indiscriminate and widespread collection of facial data to power its facial recognition tool.

98 No guidance is provided in the EU Parliament Text as to what constitutes a 'publicly accessible space'. As the phrase is not defined as 'Public space' it would tend to infer that private spaces to which the public have access are also in scope (such as retail outlets).

99 The Council Compromise Text provides more detail to this exemption and it is unamended by the EU Parliament Text: "*This Regulation shall not apply to AI*

relation to AI systems used purely for the purposes of scientific research and development[100]. There are other more specific exclusions relating to third country public authorities, law enforcement and intermediary service providers (specifically calling out that the regulation is not intended to affect other EU laws) but I don't propose to cover those in detail here[101].

High Risk AI

The "High Risk" classification for AI systems under the EU AIA falls into two categories. The first is what I have termed the "Annex II" definition.

This essentially maps AI systems to harmonised European product legislation. The relevant AI system needs to be a product in its own right, or a safety related component of a product. Typically, "*products*" as defined are those that need to undergo separate EU conformity testing before they can be launched within the EU market – due to the risks of harm if they malfunction or are not manufactured properly.

As you can imagine this is an exceptionally broad list, encompasses all general "machinery", vehicles (road, rail, water and air), toys, medical devices, PPE, lifts and radio devices to take a few examples[102].

Then you have what I refer to as the "Annex III" definitions. These refer

---

systems if and insofar placed on the market or put into service for the purpose of activities which fall outside the scope of Union law, and in any event activities concerning military, defence or national security, regardless of the type of entity carrying out those activities. In addition, this Regulation shall not apply to AI systems which are not placed on the market or put into service in the Union, where the output is used in the Union for the purpose of activities which fall outside the scope of Union law, and in any event activities concerning military, defence or national security."

100 See Article 2 6 of the Council Compromise Text

101 Article 5 in the Council Compromise Text, Articles 5a, 5b, 5c, 5d and 5 e in the EU Parliament Text

102 See Annex II in the Council Compromise Text (and the original Commission AIA Proposal)

to specific use case applications for Artificial Intelligence and are as follows:

- *Biometrics and biometrics-based systems*[103]

  This category encompasses AI systems that are designed for biometric identification or to make inferences about personal characteristics on the basis of biometric data, including systems that are designed for emotion recognition[104]. Interestingly, the latest iteration of this high risk category makes it clear that biometric ***verification*** should not be included. This is verification "*...whose sole purpose is to confirm that a specific natural person is the person he or she claims to be and to confirm the identity of a natural person for the sole purpose of having access to a service a device or premises (one to one verification).*"[105]

  Clearly this exception has been pragmatically formulated to allow biometric device unlocking, which is now in widespread global use through phone manufacturers such as Apple and Samsung, but also permits biometric verification for building access. In practical terms it may be difficult to provide a clear distinction between what is "verification" and what is "identification" in these contexts as the terms are broadly synonymous. Further guidance will also be required to distinguish these use cases from 'biometric categorisation' which has now been added as a Prohibited use case by the EU Parliament Text.[106]

---

[103] Annex III, paragraph 1

[104] See Recital 33 a (Amendment 63) of the EU Parliament Text

[105] Recital 33a (Amendment 63) ibid.

[106] See earlier discussion under Prohibited AI

- *Critical Infrastructure*[107]

  This is defined as the AI systems used as safety components in the management and operation of the supply of water, gas, heating and electricity and critical digital infrastructure. The recitals to the EU Parliament Text provide that these digital infrastructure systems are defined as "*…systems used to directly protect the physical integrity of critical infrastructure or the health and safety of persons or property*"[108]. The recital further makes it clear that systems intended to be used solely for cybersecurity purposes do not fall within the scope of this high risk classification[109].

- *Education and Vocational Training*[110]

  These are AI systems that are intended to be used for the purposes of determining access to; or materially influencing decisions on admission for places to educational and vocational institutions. As the EU Parliament Text notes, this category would include systems used to evaluate candidates for admission by testing and also those used to assess candidates' qualifications. When improperly designed, such systems can have a particularly intrusive impact on rights to education and training and may well perpetuate historic discrimination trends[111].

  The EU Parliament Text also introduces two new sub-categories in relation to AI systems that are intended to be used to assess appropriate levels of education for individuals[112] and also AI

---

107 Annex III, paragraph 2

108 Recital 34 in the EU Parliament Text (Amendment 64)

109 ibid

110 Annex III, paragraph 3

111 See Recital 35 in the EU Parliament Text (Amendment 65)

112 See Annex III, paragraph 3 (b a) (Amendment 717)

systems that are used to detect cheating during tests[113].

- *Employment, workers management and access to self-employment*[114]

  This classification is intended to capture AI systems used in employment – notably for recruitment and selection of roles; as well as decisions on promotion or termination of employment, and for task-based allocation based on individual behaviour, personal traits or biometric data[115]. This latter category having been added in the EU Parliament Text to capture the widespread use of AI powered tools by gig economy type services that assign jobs based on work patterns (such as, for example, Deliveroo or Uber).

- *Access to and enjoyment of essential private services and public services and benefits*[116]

  The essential private and public services referred to in this classification are more fully described in the EU Parliament Text recitals as healthcare services and essential services such as housing, electricity, heating/cooling, electricity and internet services. Within this category, are additionally systems that are used to evaluate credit scores and/or creditworthiness (as these decisions essentially determine eligibility for such essential services) and systems that are used to make decisions on access to health or life insurance. AI despatch systems for emergency services are also included[117]. The EU Parliament Text however specifically excludes AI systems from this category that are used for the purposes of fraud detection in the offering of financial

---

[113] See Recital 35 of the EU Parliament Text (Amendment 65)

[114] Annex III, paragraph 4

[115] See Recital 36 of the EU Parliament Text (Amendment 66)

[116] Annex III, paragraph 5

[117] Recital 37 of the EU Parliament Text (Amendment 67)

services[118].

- *Law Enforcement*[119]

  This classification encompasses a wide variety of technologies and techniques used in the context of law enforcement, including AI powered polygraphs (lie detectors), evidential quality assessments, profiling and crime analytics[120].

- *Migration, asylum and border control management*[121]

  Again, this category covers technologies used in the policing and management of asylum and border control and is analogous to the law enforcement category above[122].

- *Administration of justice and democratic processes*[123]

  Finally, there is the Administration of justice category. This is intended to cover AI systems that are used to interpret facts or law in the context of justice. The EU Parliament Text adds a new sub-category which is intended to cover systems that are "*...intended to be used for influencing the outcome of an election or referendum or the voting behaviour of natural persons...*"[124]. This is clearly a political response by EU legislators to concerns expressed in the media about attempts to influence election outcomes.

---

[118] ibid

[119] Annex III, paragraph 6

[120] Recital 37a of the EU Parliament Text (Amendment 68)

[121] Annex III paragraph 7

[122] See recital 39 of the EU Parliament Text (Amendment 70)

[123] Annex III, paragraph 8

[124] See Annex III, Paragraph 8 aa of the EU Parliament Text (Amendment 739)

Everything else

The regulation is fairly light touch when it comes to other forms of AI – Article 69 in particular encourages the adoption of codes of conduct that include the voluntary application of all of the compliance requirements specified for high risk AI in the context of other AI systems.

These codes of conduct in particular should encompass the following goals[125]:

- *Literacy*

  There should be sufficient levels of AI literacy among staff developing the AI system and users of AI systems;

- *Vulnerability*

  Providers should assess to what extent their AI systems may affect vulnerable persons or groups of persons, including children, the elderly, migrants and persons with disabilities;

- *Gender Balance and Diversity*

  Considerations need to be made about the way in which the use of such AI systems may have an impact or can increase diversity, gender balance and equality;

- *Fairness*

  Regard should be had as to whether AI systems can be used in a way that, directly or indirectly, may reinforce existing biases or inequalities;

[125] See Article 62, paragraphs 2 (a) – (g) of the EU Parliament Text (Amendment 635)

- *Representation in Development Teams*

  Providers should reflect on the need and relevance of having in place diverse development teams in view of securing an inclusive design of their systems;

- *Societal Impact*

  They should give careful consideration to whether their systems can have a negative societal impact, particularly concerning political institutions and democratic processes; and finally

- *Sustainability*

  They should evaluate how their AI systems can contribute to environmental sustainability.

Compliance Requirements for "High Risk" AI

The bulk of compliance requirements set out in the EU AIA are focused on High Risk AI (although the EU Parliament Text has introduced a new compliance category for foundation models as we have previously discussed and there are some overarching requirements in relation to transparency which I cover later on in this chapter).

Fundamental Rights Impact Assessments

One of the major criticisms directed at early drafts of the EU AIA were a lack of obligations requiring providers to benchmark systems against the impacts they were likely to cause to their users and society in general[126].

The concept of the "*impact assessment*" is now generally reflected as an accepted compliance methodology in many legislative initiatives both

126 See for example the ITechLaw publication *The EU AIA: A Green Paper Policy Analysis* (note 4, supra)

within the EU and globally to assist in the identification and mitigation of appropriate risks – see for example provisions in the GDPR on Data Protection Impact Assessments[127]. They form the basis of the UK's proposed approach to AI Governance[128] and are mentioned in the draft US Algorithmic Accountability Act[129]. It is therefore not surprising that this requirement has now been introduced by the EU Parliament Text, to complement the general principles for AI discussed earlier.

Article 29a[130] provides that prior to putting a high risk system into use (with the exception of AI systems used for critical infrastructure), the deployers of such systems are to conduct an impact assessment of the specific use context. This assessment, which is intended to cover "first use" of the relevant high risk AI system, should include the following elements, at a minimum:

- a clear outline of the intended purpose for which the system will be used;
- a clear outline of the intended geographic and temporal scope of the system's use;
- categories of natural persons and groups likely to be affected by the use of the system;
- verification that the use of the system is compliant with relevant law on fundamental rights;
- the reasonably foreseeable impact on fundamental rights of

127 Articles 35 and 36 of the EU and UK GDPR

128 See the UK AI Governance White Paper *A pro-innovation approach to AI regulation, 22 June 2023* https://www.gov.uk/government/publications/ai-regulation-a-pro-innovation-approach/white-paper

129 See https://www.congress.gov/bill/117th-congress/house-bill/6580/text

130 See Amendment 413 of the EU Parliament Text

putting the high risk AI system into use;

- specific risks of harm likely to impact marginalised persons or vulnerable groups;
- the reasonably foreseeable adverse impact of the use of the system on the environment;
- a detailed plan as to how the harms and the negative impact on fundamental rights identified will be mitigated; and
- the governance system the deployer will put in place, including human oversight, complaint-handling and redress.

Outside of first use cases, the obligation as drafted would allow deployers to draw back on previously conducted fundamental rights impact assessments.

Registration in EU wide Database

As with foundation models, all high risk AI systems are required under Article 60 to undergo registration in an EU wide database which shall be "*freely available*", "*user friendly*" and publicly accessible.[131]

Substantive High Risk Compliance Requirements

Chapter Two, Articles 8 to 16 of the EU AIA set out the key compliance requirements for high risk AI systems.

Before we get into the detail of these requirements it is perhaps worth reiterating that concerns have been expressed by AI commentators on the extent to which some of the requirements are practically achievable given the current "*state of the art*" of AI technology. We will consider particular issues as they arise in the discussion below and how these concerns have

[131] Article 60 3 (Amendment 571) of the EU Parliament Text

been addressed in the latest draft of the EU AIA.

Lifecycle Risk and Quality Management

The first is an obligation to implement and keep a risk management system going for the entire lifecycle of the relevant AI system[132]. This will entail a full evaluation of all known and foreseeable risks involved in the use of the system – both when it is used properly and in circumstances of reasonably foreseeable misuse, together with suitable risk management measures to eliminate or reduce the identified risks as far as practicable[133].

Testing and Conformity Assessments

A very important part of these compliance requirements are the testing provisions which are expressed in comprehensive terms. Article 9, paragraph 7 requires testing to be performed "*...prior to the placing on the market or the putting into service. Testing shall be made against prior defined metrics, and probabilistic thresholds that are appropriate to the intended purpose or reasonably foreseeable misuse of the high-risk AI system.*"[134]

Article 7 requires the service provider to undertake testing of the system prior to launch in the European market and this leads into full conformity assessments under Article 43 – the nature and extent of which based on the particular use case for which the high risk system will be used.

These are intended be undertaken by notified authorities in each of the member states which will determine whether or not the system is compliant, based on the quality management system and technical

132 Article 9

133 Amendments introduced by the EU Parliament Text qualify these risk management measures to those which are *technically feasible* – a pragmatic addition given concerns about the achievability of some measures phrased in earlier drafts of the measure (See Article 9 4 1 a, Amendment 269).

134 Amendment 275 of the EU Parliament Text

documentation produced, and they will issue an appropriate certificate of conformity if it is.

Finally, appropriate EU declarations of conformity under Article 48 are required to be drawn up and CE markings affixed (either physically or digitally) to conforming systems under Article 49 to show that they are compliant[135].

Data Governance

Data compliance forms a key part of this regulation. As data and datasets are the "fuel" of machine learning systems, the regulation makes it clear that training and testing datasets need to meet certain quality criteria[136] which should relate to the specific market segment in which the AI System will be used or scope of its application. The following are identified as requirements in this context[137]:

- transparency (as regards data collection purposes);
- data collection processes;
- data preparation operations (including annotation, labelling, cleaning, updating enrichment and aggregation);
- the formulation of assumptions (with respect to the information the data are supposed to represent);
- an assessment of the availability, quantity and suitability of the data sets needed;

---

135 Article 16 1 e a and 16 1 e b, Amendments 339 and 340 of the EU Parliament Text

136 Again, the EU Parliament Text qualifies these obligations by technical feasibility.

137 Article 10, 2 a a – Article 10 2 g (Amendments 280 through 287)

- examination in view of possible biases which may affect health and safety or negatively affect fundamental rights, together with appropriate mitigation measures; and

- the identification of relevant data gaps or shortcomings.

In addition, training datasets and validation and testing datasets need to be demographically appropriate for the use case (representing the right mix of people), appropriately vetted for errors and as complete as possible in view of the intended purpose of the system[138].

Finally providers are permitted exceptionally process special categories of personal data[139] in order to ensure negative bias detection and correction. This exception is subject to a number of caveats, including pseudonimisation of the data concerned; appropriate access and security measures and no transfers to third parties[140].

Technical Documentation

A comprehensive technical documentation suite is required to be maintained in relation to high risk systems before they are placed on the market and should be kept up to date[141]. The technical documentation should be drawn in such a way to demonstrate compliance with the requirements of Chapter Two of the EU AIA, providing competent authorities and notified bodies with all necessary information to assess AI system compliance.

---

138 See Article 10 3 (Amendment 288 of the EU Parliament Text)

139 See Articles 9 and 10 of the GDPR, and further Chapter Six – Big Data and Artificial Intelligence

140 Article 10 5 (Amendment 290 of the EU Parliament Text)

141 Article 11

Record Keeping (Logging by design)

Earlier versions of Article 12 of the EU AIA required that high risk AI systems should enable automatic logging of events. Such logging should ensure traceability of the AI system's functioning through its lifecycle.

This was perhaps one of the most controversial compliance requirements which was seen as technically at odds with the "black box" nature of some deep neural networks, a particular area of concern for AI commentators[142]. The EU Parliament Text again introduces an element of pragmatism by moderating this obligation by reference to the current state of the art: "*...logging capabilities shall conform to the state of the art and recognised standards or common specifications...*"[143].

The EU Parliament Text also extends this obligation to environmental issues, so that such logging should enable energy consumption monitoring, resource use and environmental impacts during the lifecycle of an applicable AI system[144].

Transparency

Article 13 provides for a requirement of transparency and provision of information. What this requires is that AI systems should be sufficiently transparent to enable users to interpret the system's output and use it appropriately – again originally a somewhat controversial requirement given the opaque nature of some AI systems, but now equally addressed pragmatically by the EU Parliament Text as follows: "*...Transparency shall thereby mean that, at the time the high-risk AI system is placed on the market, all technical means available in accordance with the generally acknowledged state of art are used to ensure that the AI system's output is*

142 See ITechLaw Green Paper *The EU AIA, A Green Paper Policy Analysis,* note 4 above

143 See Article 12 1 (Amendment 295) of the EU Parliament Text

144 Article 12 2 a (Amendment 297) of the EU Parliament Text

interpretable..."[145]

These transparency requirements also require the inclusion of intelligible instructions of use that set out the system's intended use, its level of accuracy, robustness and cyber security and all clearly known or foreseeable circumstances that could lead to risks to health and safety, fundamental rights or the environment, including by reference to illustrative examples[146]. The degree to which such systems can provide an explanation for the decisions it makes also now form part of this requirement[147].

Human Oversight

Article 14 requires that AI systems should be designed so that they can be overseen effectively by natural persons when in use[148]. This oversight should be appropriate and proportionate to the circumstances[149].

In particular there need to be "*kill switches*" to enable human operators to switch off the AI system. The EU Parliament Text adds a new exception to this which could prove to be somewhat controversial – it provides that such a kill switch should not be provided if "*...the human interference increases the risks or would negatively impact the performance in consideration of generally acknowledged state-of-the-art.*"[150]

Operators need to understand fully the limitations of such systems (demonstrating appropriate levels of AI literacy) and also need to be able to correctly interpret the output of such systems without overtly relying

145 Article 13 1 (Amendment 300) of the EU Parliament Text

146 Article 13 3 b iii (Amendment 307) of the EU Parliament Text

147 Article 13 3 b iii a (Amendment 308) of the EU Parliament Text

148 Article 14 (Amendments 314 through 320 of the EU Parliament Text

149 Article 14 4 (Amendment 317) of the EU Parliament Text

150 Article 14 4 e (Amendment 319) of the EU Parliament Text

on it and falling into the trap of "automation bias".

Robustness and Accuracy

Finally, Article 15 provides that high risk systems need to be resilient to errors faults or inconsistencies which may occur inherently within the system itself and in the environment within which it operates. They are required to embed security "*by design and default*"[151] using state of the art security measures.

Accuracy levels for such systems need to be declared and should accompany instructions for use[152].

Technical and organisational measures should be taken to ensure resilience in operation due to errors, faults or inconsistencies which may occur in operation[153].

The regulation mentions that robustness could be achieved by backup or failsafe plans and in the case of systems which continue to "learn" after being placed on the market – these need to developed in a way which avoids bias or "*feedback loops*" or mitigates them appropriately. In addition malicious manipulation of learning inputs during operation should also be addressed by mitigation measures[154].

Technical solutions to address AI vulnerabilities should include measures to "*...prevent, detect, respond to, resolve and control for attacks trying to manipulate the training dataset ('data poisoning'), or pre-trained components*

[151] Article 15 1 (Amendment 321) of the EU Parliament Text. This is a well-established EU principle which means that the relevant compliance obligation should be embedded from the very start of the design process and not "bolted on" as an afterthought

[152] This presents an interesting paradox for providers of "deep" neural networks as, given their tendency for unpredictability, so far the only pragmatic way to provide for accuracy has been through extended empirical testing

[153] Article 15 3 1 (Amendment 325) of the EU Parliament Text

[154] Article 15 3 3 (Amendment 327) of the EU Parliament Text

used in training ('model poisoning') , inputs designed to cause the model to make a mistake ('adversarial examples' or 'model evasion'), confidentiality attacks or model flaws, which could lead to harmful decision making."[155]

Obligations for Providers and Deployers of High Risk AI Systems

Article 16 reflects the obligations of providers and deployers[156] of high risk AI systems. Generally, these reflect the requirements for high risk systems discussed above.

Additional Obligations for High Risk AI Importers, Distributors and Deployers (and other third parties)

So dealing very quickly into some of the other categories of entities dealing with AI systems – it would be wrong to assume that importers and distributors of AI systems escape the draft regulation although their compliance requirements are somewhat more straightforward than those reflected in Article 16 above.

Generally speaking these provisions[157] consist of information, verification and identification requirements – ensuring that the relevant provider has complied with its obligations. The deployers of high risk AI systems are tasked predominantly with ensuring that appropriate levels of human oversight, monitoring use and maintaining data set quality and logs to the extent they have control over those aspects of the system's operation[158].

Article 28 sets out the conditions for treating such a party as a provider in their own right (if for example they market a high risk system under

155 Article 15 4 (Amendment 329) of the EU Parliament Text

156 A concept introduced by the EU Parliament Text. Deployers are referred to in previous versions of the EU AIA as "Users"

157 See Articles 26, 27, 28 and 29

158 See Article 29

their own brand or trademark[159] or make a substantial modification to a high risk system that has already been placed on the market such that it remains a high risk system[160] or substantially modify a system such that it becomes a high risk system when not previously classified as one[161]).

The EU Parliament Text additionally in this context provides for a new Article which prevents the imposition of unfair contractual terms on SMEs or startups[162]. This is presumably to address the size imbalance in the industry between major organisations that develop and launch AI systems and the wider eco-system of smaller companies using or relying on such systems in the provision of their services. The net effect of such a provision is to prevent the burden of compliance (and penalties under the measure) from being shifted unfairly to those smaller entities.

Transparency

Article 52 contains a distinct and separate transparency obligation which is intended to apply to all AI systems, whatever the category, to the extent they are intended to interact with human users[163].

This provision is designed to prevent a scenario where human users are "tricked" into believing they are dealing with another human, when in fact they are dealing with a machine – a situation which is all too prevalent now for example in the context of dealing with call centres.

The EU Parliament Text expands the obligation to include "*...which functions are AI enabled, if there is human oversight, and who is responsible for the decision-making process, as well as the existing rights and processes that, according to ... law, allow natural persons or their representatives to*

159 Article 28 1 a (Amendment 392) of the EU Parliament Text

160 Article 28 1 b (Amendment 393) of the EU Parliament Text

161 Article 28 1 b a (Amendment 394) of the EU Parliament Text

162 See new Article 28a (Amendment 398) of the EU Parliament Text

163 Confusingly, these are distinct from the high risk transparency requirements of Article 13 discussed previously

object against the application of such systems to them and to seek judicial redress against decisions taken by or harm caused by AI systems, including their right to seek an explanation." [164]

Similarly, declarations are required (and consent is required to be obtained) for emotion recognition systems (such as those typically deployed by recruiters to detect involuntary responses when a candidate is being interviewed).[165]

Deepfake content is also subject to such declarations, but this is now subject to an exemption in relation to content which "*...forms part of an evidently creative, satirical, artistic or fictional cinematographic, video games visuals and analogous work or programme...*"[166].

These provisions do not apply in the context of law enforcement.

Regulatory Sandboxes

Lastly on the innovation side, Article 53 provides for what are termed "*regulatory sandboxes*".

What these are in essence are controlled environments which member states can set up to enable the testing and development of innovative AI systems under active supervision by regulators, before they are actually placed on the market.

This approach has been trialled quite successfully in other contexts by local EU regulators – for example the UK Financial Conduct Authority prior to Brexit ran, and continues to run, regulatory sandboxes for innovative financial services products.

---

[164] Article 52 1 (Amendment 484) of the EU Parliament Text

[165] Article 52 2 (Amendment 485) of the EU Parliament Text

[166] Article 52 3a (Amendment 487) of the EU Parliament Text

Governance and Regulation

The latest version of the AIA as set out in the EU Parliament Text provides for a new independent pan-European AI regulator, the AI Office, which is intended to have full legal personality[167].

The AI Office is clearly envisaged by the European Parliament to have a degree of arms' length separation from the Commission, a criticism levelled at prior proposals which were comprised an AI board that was mandated to provide advice and assistance to the Commission. Generally it is mandated to provide a central co-ordinating function for national competent authorities, and its major duties will include monitoring compliance with the regulation across the EU, mediating internal disagreements between EU authorities, collecting expertise and best practice amongst EU member states and publishing an annual report indicating levels of compliance and serious incidents[168].

Penalties

Much has been written and commented upon in relation to the potential penalties that are exerciseable by the European authorities in the event of a breach of the Artificial Intelligence Act, and it is probably worthwhile covering these in a short discussion here.

The first point to note is that the draft regulation essentially "*piggybacks*" AI compliance onto the proactive market surveillance regime (referred to as post market monitoring) which already exists for product compliance within Europe. These are the overarching mechanisms which ensure product safety and compliance with appropriate standards.

The regulation also includes comprehensive mechanisms to allow regulators access to full system data and documentation – which may

---

167 See Article 56 (Amendment 525) of the EU Parliament text

168 The comprehensive list of related obligations and duties is set out in Article 56 (as amended)

include training datasets and source code pertaining to the AI model itself.

Obviously, these disclosure powers are likely to prove highly controversial for service providers given that some of the intellectual property involved will be inherently valuable and protected by trade secrets.

AI systems can be withdrawn from the EU market directly, or prohibited from use, or specific corrective actions can be specified and prescribed within a defined period.

And if all else fails, there are the ultimate sanction of administrative fines – as currently drafted at the following levels:

- 40,000,000 euros or 7% of worldwide turnover for breaches of Article 5 on prohibited use[169];

- 20,000,000 euros or 4% of worldwide turnover for breaches of Article 10 (data and data governance) and 13 (transparency)[170];

- 10,000,000 euros or 2% of worldwide turnover for non-compliance by an AI system or foundation model with ***any*** requirement under the AIA (other than Articles 5, 10 and 13 above)[171]; and

- 5,000,000 euros or 1% of worldwide turnover for the supply of incorrect, incomplete or misleading information to notified bodies and national competent authorities.

[169] Article 71 3 (Amendment 647) of the EU Parliament Text

[170] Again, it should be pointed out that this is not to be confused with the Article 52 transparency requirement

[171] Article 71 4 (Amendment 651) of the EU Parliament Text

The EU AI Liability Directive

When original Commission AIA Proposal was published, there was some criticism that the measure did not in fact include any private rights of action for European consumers harmed by the actions of "rogue" artificial intelligence systems[172].

In what is perhaps a response to such criticism, on 28th September 2022, the EU Commission published a draft companion measure to the Artificial Intelligence Act, the AI Liability Directive ("AI LD").

As this companion measure is framed as a directive (rather than a regulation), it will require national implementing laws for it to come into force. The Commission explained its rationale for adopting a directive approach rather than a regulation in this context in its explanatory notes: "*…A directive is the most suitable instrument for this proposal, as it provides the desired harmonisation effect and legal certainty, while also providing the flexibility to enable Member States to embed the harmonised measures without friction into their national liability regimes.*"[173]

The AI LD applies to providers of high risk AI systems (as defined in the EU AIA) and Users[174] of such systems located in the EU. This very closely mirrors, understandably, the compliance hierarchy set out in the AI Act itself.

It enhances the rights of private claimants in three ways –

[172] See for example the ITechLaw Green Paper referred to at note 4 above

[173] ***Proposal for a DIRECTIVE OF THE EUROPEAN PARLIAMENT AND OF THE COUNCIL ON ADAPTING NON-CONTRACTUAL CIVIL LIABILITY RULES TO ARTIFICIAL INTELLIGENCE****, COM/2022/496 final*, see: https://commission.europa.eu/system/files/2022-09/1_1_197605_prop_dir_ai_en.pdf

[174] These terms are intended to align with those in the EU AIA. As "users" as a concept have now been superseded by "deployers" it likely that this reference in the AI LD will also be amended.

Firstly, the AI LD introduces a right of access to evidence[175]. This is less of an innovative measure for those countries that already have disclosure and/or discovery rights in litigation – but there are a surprising number of countries in the EU that do not allow for this right in their litigation processes.

Secondly, it introduces a rebuttable presumption of non-compliance as against the provider where it fails to disclose or preserve relevant evidence at its disposal[176] , thus ruling ineffective tactics of passive non-compliance.

Finally, it introduces a rebuttable presumption of causality[177] so that instead of the victim having to prove that the relevant AI system caused the loss complained of (which would be the normal evidential burden in cases of this nature), the AI provider needs to rebut a presumption that its system did cause the damage.

This is a response to the complexity of modern AI systems and the time, effort and costs that litigants would have to face proving causation, a significant concern expressed by EU legislators.

---

175 Article 3 paragraphs 1-4, AI LD

176 Article 3 paragraph 5 AI LD

177 Article 4 AI LD

CHAPTER SIX

BIG DATA AND ARTIFICIAL INTELLIGENCE

It is of course, big data that sits at the heart of artificial intelligence.

As computing systems generally have grown in power and capacity, so the consumption of data has grown exponentially. One of the most exciting developments of machine learning is its ability to analyse data in vastly more dimensions than human beings have ever been able to, at a far quicker pace. This ability to spot unexpected correlations and patterns in data is incredibly powerful and has already provided some very surprising applications – one US insurance start up[178] for example can analyse a "selfie" using thousands of different facial data points to determine how quickly an individual is ageing, their gender, body mass index and whether they smoke. Their system predicts life expectancy of individuals much more accurately than traditional methods. Another system developed by researchers at Stanford University can apparently (and somewhat controversially) identify an individual's sexuality by identifying or correlating a complex series of facial characteristics[179]. Even more outlandishly, there is a machine learning system it is claimed can reconstruct a reasonable facsimile of someone's face from the sound of their voice[180].

---

178 Lapetus Solutions Inc.

179 https://osf.io/zn79k/ "Deep Neural Networks are more accurate than humans in detecting sexual orientation from facial images", Wang, Kosinski, 2017

180 This is *Speech2Face*, a deep neural network created by MIT researchers. See https://www.onartificialintelligence.com/articles/17429/ai-generates-human-faces-based-on-their-voices

Not unsurprisingly, the potential for such AI solutions to have a significant impact on personal life and privacy has drawn the attention of legislators and is a feature of the General Data Protection Regulation (or "GDPR") which we'll look at shortly. Before we do this however, and in order to provide a framework for our analysis, it is worth describing how machine learning systems acquire and generate data and typically how they process such data.

It should also be pointed out that the data acquisition and manipulation features of AI systems are not unique to this technology but are amplified to an extreme degree by machine learning. Analytics are very much a product of the complex data producing society that we now live in.

For the most part we tend to think of the handing over of data (including personal data) to third parties as a conscious transaction which we positively have to provide our pro-active consent for. In fact, this is an outmoded view of reality. In many cases now, data (some of which will inevitably be "personal") is generated automatically by the variety of "smart" devices we interact with. Indeed, we don't even need to actively interact with a device for data to be generated about us. We could be the subjects of a facial recognition system at an airport or have our mobile phones queried by MAC and other network "sniffers" without even being aware of it. Indeed, this is one of the ways Covid-19 "*Track and Trace*" apps function. Your phone acts as a geolocator and identifies whether or not you have been in close contact with an infected person.

Predictive Analytics

The Information Accountability Foundation (IAF) has identified four types of data that form the basis of data analytics[181] – that is to say multiple items of data which in broad terms together disclose a *pattern* (ie typically of usage or consumption in terms of a particular device or movement in terms of surveillance etc.). These types of data are

[181] "The origins of personal data and its implications for governance", OECD March 2014

"*Provided*" data (as described above) the most traditional means – that data that is consciously given by individuals. "*Observed*" data might be data drawn from surveillance systems. "*Derived*" data is data drawn directly from other sources to produce new classes of data, and "*Inferred*" data is produced typically by analysis of existing data to make predictions. It is this last class of data which are referred to as predictive data analytics (or more simply *predictive analytics*) where machine learning systems have been making ever impressive technological advances.

The most immediate influence of this is best illustrated by the systemic impact predictive analytics are having on the insurance industry, which has been quick to embrace their potential. Quite apart from the jobs impact in relation to claims handling and processing, the technology is transforming the way in which insurance companies model risk and hence price premiums.

At its most simple level, insurers model risk by way of a concept known as "*pooling*". Insurers put large groups of similar people together, using common risk modelling points, and their premiums are used to fund a "common pool". In any given year, some will need to be paid out and some will not. As long as the common pool remains liquid – the system continues to work. Insurance based predictive analytics function by giving insurers more detail about individuals and associated risks. This allows for far more accurate risk pricing and removes the need to pool broad groups of people together.

Obviously this gives rise to a whole host of ethical questions about the availability and pricing of insurance as the technology leads us down the path of what has been referred to as "micro" pooling of insurance risk.

Car driving behaviours monitored by so called telematics "under the hood" black boxes are one obvious example which could lead to "risky" behaviours driving up insurance pricing and "safe" behaviours lowering it. Even more serious is the impact of advanced analytics on genetic data which might model susceptibility to genetic disease and therefore impact the pricing and availability of life insurance coverage.

Data Acquisition

Aside from predictive analytics, machine learning systems have a prodigious capacity to self-generate, collect and of course exchange data whilst they are being used (indeed, some devices, such as autonomous and semi-autonomous vehicles) are pro-actively designed on this basis. What the IAF neglects to include in its analysis is also the category of "*Generated*" data, although this might arguably fall within their category of "*Observed*" data.

Data generation, acquisition and exchange has already drawn the significant attention of regulators. The European Commission recently published its *Strategy on Co-Operative Intelligent Transport Systems or "CIT-S"*[182] which sets out its approach to developing a standardised intelligent transport infrastructure allowing vehicles to communicate with each other, with centralised traffic management systems and other highway users[183]. The potential for such data to be misused is clearly troubling – for example not only could a CAV identify a journey destination, it could also potentially also report back on driving habits (when not in autonomous mode) and theoretically identify any traffic offences.

In the context of our discussion such data could obviously also have an impact on the manner in which insurance is offered to the user of the vehicle when under human control.

To date, the policy adopted by the EU Commission has been to identify such data as personal data and therefore afford it the protection of the European data protection framework.

182 See http://ec.europa.eu/energy/sites/ener/files/documents/1_en_act_part1_v5.pdf

183 Unfortunately plans to implement an EU wide Regulation embodying the principles of the CIT-S strategy have to date stalled, with the EU Council and Parliament objecting to the draft measure on the basis of its perceived lack of technological neutrality

Understanding how AI systems Process Data

We tend to think of traditional computer data processing as the assimilation of large amounts of data which are then varied/changed/updated or adapted in some mechanistic way to support the application or program being utilised by the system.

In contrast, as I indicated in the introduction to this book and at the start of this particular chapter, the inherent value in most AI systems is in their ability to spot patterns, correlations and different dimensionalities in the data sets which they observe. Whilst this may not have a hugely practical consequence so far as the regulatory definitions of "*personal data*"[184] and "*processing*"[185] are concerned, it is conceptually important to understand this difference and it is a topic we will return to in the context of intellectual property and artificial intelligence later on in this book.

AI systems tend to observe, learn and model from the large data sets they are exposed to. The value in the utility of such systems is not therefore just in the sense that they can process the data elements in large data sets – it is also in their ability to spot and correlate patterns in such data and learn (or optimise output) through use of the *Learner* element of the system.

The closest analogy is of course a human being learning a new skill. A human will assimilate a skill from tangible materials (data) and training. Irrespective of whether those tangible materials (ie. the data elements) are returned to a third party, lost or subsequently destroyed, the skill and knowhow (or *learned* behaviours) still remain with the person.

---

[184] Article 4(1) GDPR

[185] Article 4(2) GDPR

The General Data Protection Regulation ("GDPR")

The GDPR ushered in a new era of responsibilities for those who control or process the personal data of EU citizens, and rights for those who are the subjects of such processing. Unfortunately, in pursuing the undoubtedly noble cause of protecting individual citizens the measure, as we shall see in a moment, has also created significant difficulties for the implementers users and owners of artificially intelligent systems – creating a "*Gordian knot*" of regulatory hurdles which often seem to be completely at odds with the practical implications (and business case benefits) of using such systems.

I do not propose in this section to provide a comprehensive guide to the measure which is far reaching beyond the confines of the immediate subject matter – but rather provide a view as to the issues which you will need to be aware of from a practical and conceptual basis when looking at AI systems that are designed to process personal data.

It goes without saying that machine learning systems which do not process personal data are outside the scope of the legislation – however it pays to remember that personal data is not confined merely to data which refers *directly* or *overtly* to a living individual – the definition is wide enough to encompass data which could achieve such status through a process of *indirect* inference or derivation (see my previous comments under the heading of predictive analytics).

Key Concepts

Before we examine the impact of the GDPR on the users, implementers and owners of artificially intelligent computer systems, it is worth stepping through a few of the concepts which will define our debate. As before, this section will be necessarily led by the focus of this book – that is to say issues which are created or caused by artificial intelligence technologies.

"Fair" processing

At its heart, the GDPR mandates that all personal data should be processed *fairly*. Article 5(1)(a) provides that personal data must be "*processed fairly, lawfully and in a transparent manner in relation to the data subject.*" As we have seen previously, it is the inherent complexity and "black box" nature of many AI system structures and architectures that causes considerable difficulties in the context of liability and causation. The position is no different in the context of data protection.

At its heart, the concept of fairness is driven by compliance with the Data Protection Principles[186] (which are largely unchanged from the prior regime under the Data Protection Directive) including the concept of transparency.

Transparency is a theme which runs through this narrative and in this context self-evidently refers to the manner in which the processing is publicised and clear to the data subject. This requirement generally refers to the purposes for which personal data are to be utilised, but as we shall see in a little more detail later, it *also* refers to the way in which such data is *computationally* processed by the AI system.

Generally speaking, the requirement of transparency is achieved procedurally under the GDPR by reference to the provision of "*fair processing*" or privacy information notices to the affected data subjects stating (*inter alia*) who the relevant parties are who will be controlling and processing their information, for what purposes it will be processed and who such data is going to be shared with. This however is but the starting point for such notices. There are significant practical and procedural difficulties applying this process to machine learning technologies, particularly given that the GDPR is much more prescriptive about how such notices should be designed and what they should (and should not) achieve, more of which we discuss below.

186 Article 5 (1) GDPR

Data Processors or Data Controllers?

As with any technological system which makes use of Personal Data, the providers and users of machine learning systems need to evaluate the extent to which they are Processors or Controllers of the personal data used by the system.

It is not the purpose of this book to provide a detailed explanation of each of these concepts but broadly speaking a Controller is a natural or legal person who determines the purposes and means of the data processing[187] and a Processor is a natural or legal person who processes personal data on behalf of the Controller[188]. Often in the case of machine learning systems, the analysis as to whether the provider of the system is a Joint Controller with the user (rather than a Processor) can become quite complex issue to determine, particularly where personal data are ingested into a machine learning model as part of a training dataset to improve that system's output. Very often the answer is highly context specific and can hinge on issues such as the extent to which the model is intended to be used for purposes additional to the original ones commissioned[189], or whether it is dedicated to a single use case.

Consent vs. Legitimate Interests

The lawfulness or otherwise of the relevant processing is also central to the regulatory framework. For the purposes of this debate, this will largely be driven by two of the concepts listed in Article 6 of the GDPR – either that "*the data subject has given consent to the processing of his or her personal data*"[190] or the "*processing is necessary for the purposes of the legitimate interests pursued by the controller... except where such interests are overridden*

[187] Article 4(7)

[188] Article 4(8)

[189] Such as for example, where a supplier intends to use a model trained on data provided by one customer for its other customers

[190] Article 6(1)a

by the interests or fundamental rights and freedoms of the data subject which require protection of personal data..."

Under the data protection regime prior to the introduction of the GDPR, consent of the data subject had become somewhat of a discredited concept – many businesses had adopted the approach of burying general consent deep in a raft of obscure terms and conditions, or pre-populating check boxes, forcing data subjects to proactively "uncheck" in order *not* to give consent. Again, European legislators have effectively blocked these practices under the GDPR and strengthen the concept, stating that "*...Consent should be given by a clear affirmative act establishing a freely given specific, informed and unambiguous indication of the data subject's agreement as to the processing of personal data...this could include...conduct which clearly indicates in this context the data subject's acceptance of the proposed processing of his personal data. Silence, pre-ticked boxes or inactivity should not therefore constitute consent.*"[191]. The natural corollary of this of course is that the individual data subject is free to withdraw such consent at any time – indeed this is the position that is legislated for in Article 7(3) of the GDPR.

For the purposes of our current analysis, and indeed generally in relation to all personal data processing based on this ground, it does of course mean that consent as a lawful basis for processing has been dramatically reduced in utility – on any objective basis, why go to the trouble of obtaining pro-active consent for processing in relation to a particular purpose – including significant levels of investment in systems and technology to carry out such activity if consent can be withdrawn at any time by any individual?

This practical problem with pro-active consent has meant that may businesses are now seeking to rely on *legitimate interests* instead as a lawful processing ground. It is this sea change in approach which is fuelling a healthy growth in GDPR audit assessment activity – because simply put,

[191] See Recital 32 of the GDPR

if a business seeks to rely on their *legitimate interests*, they must undertake a comprehensive and detailed assessment[192] which balances these interests with the rights and interests of the data subjects concerned. The point here is that the processing must be *necessary* for the data controller's legitimate interests, and not merely *convenient.* Article 13(1)d of the GDPR provides that where a data controller is relying on the legitimate interests ground, it must explain this in the relevant privacy information notice.

Profiling

Article 4(4) of the GDPR introduces the concept of "*profiling*" which will be of particular relevance to the use of AI systems evaluating and making decisions on data sets comprised of large amounts of personal data. This provides that profiling means "*any form of automated processing of personal data consisting of the use of personal data to evaluate certain aspects relating to a natural person, in particular to analyse or predict aspects concerning that natural person's performance at work, economic situation, health, personal preferences, interests, reliability, behaviour, location or movements*".

The three key aspects of the profiling process are that it should be automated; carried out using personal data and utilised to evaluate personal aspects of a natural person. It is clear that the legislators intended this concept to be construed as widely as possible[193], so that whilst the decision making involved has to include some form of automated processing, it does not rule out human intervention per se. Equally speaking, profiling does not need to involve the higher predictive elements of a machine learning system – it can e.g. simply entail the classification of people in terms of their gender, race and interests.

---

192 A so-called "DPIA" or Data Protection Impact Assessment

193 See the Article 29 Working Party paper entitled "Guidelines on Automated individual decision making and Profiling for the purposes of Regulation 2016/679 (3 October 2017)

Automated Decision Making

Article 22(1) introduces another key concept, that of automated decision making. This may or may not include profiling but is distinguished from the former as being performed solely by machine (ie with no human intervention).

The GDPR includes a right for data subjects "*not to be subject to a decision which is based solely on automated processing, including profiling, which produces legal effects concerning him or her or similarly significantly affects him or her.*" The key point here is that if the automated decision making falls within the definition set out in Article 22, then legitimate interests cannot be used as a lawful processing ground and the redefined concept of consent, with all of its inherent weaknesses (at least from a business perspective), needs to be used instead. It is important to note however that not all machine learning decisions will be caught by this definition. There are several additional considerations to be taken into account before the Article 22 threshold is reached.

Solely Automated

The first requirement is that the automated decision making or profiling needs to be "*solely automated*". What this means is that there is effectively no human involvement in the decision making or profiling process. In the world of big data this is a substantial concern for those businesses that work on a large scale. Artificially intelligent systems have the ability to substantially increase processing speed whilst retaining sophistication in the assessments applied to such decisions. Without commenting on the socio-political and ethical aspects of such an approach, this is an undoubted technological advantage for those citizens who ultimately benefit and for whom the outcome would otherwise be delayed.

There has been much debate about what level of human "in the loop" involvement there needs to be to avoid this requirement and some clues are provided by the original Article 29 Working Party on this particular topic. In essence human involvement needs to be *meaningful*, as they state "*the controller cannot avoid the Article 22 provisions by fabricating human involvement*"[194].

Clearly, human involvement cannot be tokenised. It should be carried out by someone who has the authority to review and if necessary reverse that decision and who can also weigh all available data supporting it[195]. Care also needs to be given to natural human biases in this situation as well. This was considered by the UK's Information Commissioner in a 2019 AI related blog post[196], where the concepts of automation bias and lack of interpretability were considered as potential indicators which could cause a system to fall within the "*solely automated*" category.

Automation Bias

Automation bias refers to the natural human tendency to trust the outputs of models based on mathematics and data. The argument runs that in trusting such technologies, humans become complacent and stop using their own judgment to evaluate and assess outputs. In essence this is the paradigm expressed in comedic terms by the phrase "*Computer says no*"[197]

Lack of Interpretability

Lack of interpretability in essence refers to the characteristics discussed elsewhere in this book of deep neural networks – that is to say their "black box" characteristics. The very fact that a human might find such a system difficult to interpret or challenge, because it cannot be easily understood,

---

194 Guidelines on Automated individual decision-making and Profiling for the purposes of Regulation 2016/679, adopted 3rd October 2017

195 Guidelines on Automated individual decision-making and Profiling for the purposes of Regulation 2016/679, adopted 3rd October 2017, page 21

196 Automated Decision Making: the role of meaningful human reviews see: https://ico.org.uk/about-the-ico/news-and-events/ai-blog-automated-decision-making-the-role-of-meaningful-human-reviews/

197 First coined in the 2004 BBC TV comedy series *Little Britain*

could lead it to become 'solely automated'.

Legal Effects

In addition to the 'solely automated' requirement, the automated decision making or profiling needs to have "legal effects" on the data subject concerned – these are relatively straightforward to categorise – they refer to decisions that impact the legal rights, status or rights under a contract of the affected data subject. The Article 29 Working Party provides examples of this such as the cancellation of contracts, denial of social benefit payments or even refusal of admission to a country[198].

Similarly Significant [Effects]

It is important to note however that the automated decision or profiling does not necessarily need to produce legal effects on a data subject to fall within its scope. Article 22 provides, somewhat inelegantly, that it can apply in circumstances where the decision "*similarly significantly affects him or her.*" For ease of reference, I have referred to this impact as "Similarly Significant Effects".

What then are Similarly Significant Effects? These are outcomes which are broadly equivalent in their impact to legal effects. The concern of the legislators here is to protect data subjects from being prejudiced by automated decisions which will fundamentally affect them. Remember also that this analysis should not necessarily be confined solely to "*obtained*" data – it could also apply to data that has been "*derived*" or "*inferred*" – that is to say correlated indirectly without being proactively handed over by the data subject concerned.

Again the Article 29 Working Party provides useful examples[199] such as the automatic refusal of an online credit application or e-recruiting

---

198 Guidelines on Automated individual decision-making and Profiling for the purposes of Regulation 2016/679, adopted 3rd October 2017, page 21

199 Ibid.

practices without human intervention. The decisions themselves need to have the potential to "*...significantly affect the circumstances, behaviour or choices of the individuals concerned; have a prolonged or permanent impact on the data subject; or at [their] most extreme, lead to the exclusion or discrimination of individuals...*"[200].

Very significantly (and perhaps even more problematically for our purposes) *Similiarly Significant Effects* are judged by reference to their subjective impact on the data subject and not by means of a generalised objective view of how they might have such impact (***not*** in other words the archetypal "*man on the Clapham omnibus*"[201]). So for example, someone who is in a minority group, disabled, or is a child might be impacted more significantly than an able-bodied person or an adult[202]. Quite how this impact could be modelled on an operational basis for the purposes of AI systems remains largely unresolved.

Special Category Data

Finally, the concept of Special Category Data as that is defined in Article 9 of the GDPR needs to be considered, to the extent that this is relevant. Special Category Data are defined as the protected characteristics of an individual[203], including their race, ethnic origin, genetic data, biometric data (when used for identification), health and sexual characteristics. The processing of these classes of personal data trigger enhanced protections under the GDPR due to their sensitivity, which generally prohibits any such activity unless certain limited exceptions apply, including as in the case of automated decision making, the explicit consent of the data

---

200 Ibid.

201 This is the hypothetical '*ordinary reasonable person*' standard adopted in many cases by English common law (see *Hall v. Brooklands Auto Racing Club* [1933] 1 KB 205

202 Guidelines on Automated individual decision-making and Profiling for the purposes of Regulation 2016/679, adopted 3rd October 2017, page 22

203 See Article 9 (1)

subject.

Clearly, use of Special Category Data are a particular legal concern for applications such as Automated Facial Recognition, particularly given the new provisions of the Artificial Intelligence Act, which also regulates collection and use of biometric derived data[204]. I discuss some of the more specific concerns arising from use of facial recognition systems in Chapter Seven. For the specific purposes of this chapter however, it is important to remember that Special Category Data can also be subject to automated decision making and profiling under Article 22 of the GDPR.

Purpose limitation and data minimisation

The concepts covered by Articles 5(1)(b) and 5(1)(c) of the GDPR, which continue with the so called "*purpose limitation*" and "*data minimisation*" principles are also potential hurdles to the implementation of certain classes of machine learning systems. They explicitly provide that personal data should be "*collected for specified and legitimate purpose and not further processed in a manner which is incompatible with those purposes*" and it should also be "*adequate, relevant and limited to what is necessary in relation to the purposes for which they are processed*".

As we discussed earlier, it is self-evident that these requirements *could* potentially impede the use of unsupervised machine learning (the so called Rumsfeldian "*unknown knowns*"[205]) in a big data context. Such systems generate potentially useful analysis or correlation of data sets in circumstance that could not reasonably have been predicted or anticipated at the outset (such as the example quoted at the beginning of this chapter in relation to facial characteristics leading to a correlation in sexuality).

[204] See Chapter Five for a fuller discussion of the proposed AIA provisions on biometrics

[205] Also referred to (and potentially inspired by) a poem by D.H. Lawrence – *New Heaven and Earth*

Privacy by Design

The final concept that is worth discussing in this section is that of "*privacy by design*". This approach, which is mandated by the GDPR[206], was not a requirement of the prior Data Protection Directive. Encouragingly, it is this principle which may assist the users and owners of machine learning systems that have a personal data impact.

What privacy by design (technically "*privacy by design and privacy by default*") requires is a structured design approach when creating a new information processing system. This means enshrining the concept of data privacy at its heart, rather than bolting it on as an afterthought which is so often the case in system architecture design. Often this will entail a root and branch analysis of the operational and ethical reasons why the personal data are needed and a full understanding of the impact of such data collection on the potential data subjects. The Privacy Commissioner of Ontario in Canada has published what is widely regarded as the leading conceptual approach in achieving privacy by design, by setting out seven foundational principles which should be at the heart of any such approach[207].

A first step on the path towards achieving privacy by design in a data context is by use of what are known as Privacy Impact Assessments (or DPIAs) (which are not to be confused with Privacy information notices). Article 35 of the GDPR provides that "*Where a type of processing in particular using new technologies, and taking into account the nature, scope, context and purposes of the processing, is likely to result in a high risk to the rights and freedoms of natural persons, the Controller shall, prior to the*

[206] Article 25 GDPR

[207] See *Privacy by Design, A Primer by the Ontario Privacy Commissioner*. Broadly speaking the seven principles accord with the general approach outlined above – by defining e.g. a proactive, not a reactive approach, making privacy a default setting, embedding privacy into the solution design, applying a positive sum (not a zero sum) approach, providing for full lifecycle protection, keeping use of data visible and transparent and ensuring respect for user privacy

processing, carry out an assessment of the impact of the envisaged processing operations on the protection of personal data."[208]

Interestingly, as we have seen, this type of impact assessment methodology is now forming part of nascent AI regulation in its own right – so the draft EU Artificial Intelligence Act now requires what are referred to as fundamental rights impact assessments[209], and the UK draft AI Governance White Paper, although proposing a very different regulatory regime to that of the EU AIA also validates these assessments as a vital compliance tool[210].

Understanding information flows – what is collected and when, how it stored and for what purposes and how such data is computationally processed through the relevant system are a key part of such analysis. As we have previously discussed, any difficulties in explaining the computational processes of a "*black box*" AI system will therefore need to be balanced very carefully with cogent, ethical and logical reasons for such collection and processing, which can significantly justify the benefits of using such a system for the relevant data processing application.

Privacy information notices

All of this brings us back to the GDPR requirement that we discussed at the beginning of this chapter of ensuring *transparency* in processing by use of privacy information or "*fair processing*" notices.

As you will recall, these are required whether a business is seeking to rely on the *legitimate interests* or *consent* ground for lawful processing. Whilst admirable as a concept, such notices have the potential to create substantial difficulties in the context of artificial intelligence and machine learning, especially bearing in mind the complexity and "*black box*"

[208] Article 35(1) GDPR

[209] See Chapter Five

[210] See Chapter Fourteen

nature of such systems.

Articles 12, 13 and 14 of the GDPR provide a particularly clear example of the potentially irreconcilable tautologies involved, by stipulating on the one hand that such notices should be "...*concise, transparent, intelligible and easily accessible...using clear and plain language...*"[211] whilst on the other hand stating that where automated decision making and/or profiling is involved that "...*meaningful information about the logic involved...*"[212] is also supplied. This is evidently not an easy tightrope to negotiate – particularly in a machine learning context. The logical first approach might be to provide a detailed explanation for the data subject setting out the context and grounds for the processing and explaining in detail the computational details of the AI system being used, however this is likely to have the opposite effect of confusing the data subject or overloading them with information. Indeed, the Article 29 Working Party has specifically stated that "*information fatigue*" should be avoided[213].

The EU Artificial Intelligence Act, as we have seen, now proposes to overlay additional transparency requirements for certain classes of AI system[214]. For AI systems that also use personal data and are targeted for use within the European Union (or by EU citizens), this raises the prospect of another compliance tier to achieve, a not insignificant hurdle.

With perhaps a nod to this tautology (at least so far as the GDPR is concerned), the framers of the legislation have indicated that there are various mechanisms which can be used to highlight in a user-friendly way, the information which is required to be conveyed to the users of

---

211 Article 12(1) GDPR

212 Articles 13(2)(f) and 14(2)(g) GDPR

213 See Paragraph 7 of the Article 29 Working Party paper on Transparency 17/EN WP260

214 See in particular Article 13 of the AIA (discussed in Chapter Five)

such systems.

The first accessible method which could be used is to implement clear iconography (on the basis that 'a picture is worth a thousand words') into the relevant privacy information notice. The use of icons is not a new approach, however the key has been to develop a consistent set of symbols which have an apparent individual meaning and read consistently with each other – often easier said than done. The GDPR provides a mechanism for the introduction of standardised icons under Article 12(8), but as yet there are no agreed forms.

The second method is very much context driven and depends upon the nature of the system involved and the manner in which personal data are to be collected. It is however of relevance to complex information processing systems and relies on making relevant information available to the data subject when it is needed, rather than in one large undigestible notice up front. "*Just in time*" notices (as they are referred to) rely on statements on information processing being given at the time a relevant question is being asked of an individual (through the use e.g. of pop-up or pop-over dialogue boxes). These can be coupled with an approach with allows for "*layering*" – basic information being made available with a "*click through*" link for those users who desire to have access to more detailed information about the manner in which their data will be processed.

It does not take a lot of imagination to see that innovative adoption of these techniques (which whilst potentially difficult to conceptualise at the outset), may provide implementers of machine learning systems with a route through the potentially conflicting requirements of Articles 12, 13 & 14 of the GDPR, and now the additional requirements of the AIA.

The Data Protection Act 2018

The UK's separation from the European Union, or Brexit as it has commonly become known, adds unfortunately another degree of complexity to what is an undoubtedly a difficult legislative context to navigate for the users of machine learning systems. It is important to bear in mind that, where previously they were closely aligned, the UK and EU are now on very diverging paths so far as data related AI regulation is concerned.

The new Data Protection Act (the "DPA 2018"), which was enacted into law synchronously with the General Data Protection Regulation on May 25th 2018, aims to enshrine the essential principles of the GDPR into UK law post-Brexit. Sadly, the post-Brexit legislative map for data in the UK is somewhat confused now, as the position is governed not only by the DPA 2018, but also by what is termed the 'UK GDPR'. Essentially a parallel version of the EU GDPR which has been adjusted to conform to UK domestic law[215]. It is beyond the scope of this work to delve into the complexities of the interaction between these measures, however it is worth highlighting a couple of measures in the DPA 2018.

Unfortunately, in the legislators' assiduous attempts to "*gold plate*" the UK's data protection compliance (no doubt fostered by a desire to attain equivalence with the remaining member states of the EU in terms of data transfers), the measure includes some criminal sanctions for companies and somewhat more worryingly, personal criminal sanctions for company directors. Whilst the Act does not provide for custodial sentences on breach (the sanctions are in essence limited to fines), these new offences will no doubt add a degree of real anxiety, given the irreconcilable tautologies in the GDPR we have discussed above, to those who seek to use and implement machine learning solutions in a post-Brexit environment.

It is worthwhile considering two in particular that have been introduced in relation to personal data and understanding their potential implications for artificial intelligence.

---

215 The relevant amendments are made by s3 of the European Union (Withdrawal) Act 2018

Unlawful obtaining of personal data

The Act provides in section 170 that *"it is an offence for a person knowingly or recklessly (a) to obtain or disclose personal data without the consent of the controller, (b) to procure the disclosure of personal data to another person without the consent of the controller, or (c) after obtaining personal data, to retain it without the consent of the person who was the controller in relation to the personal data when it was obtained."*[216]. Sub-sections (1) and (2) provide for various defences, including in relation to the prevention or detection of crime; for the purposes of law or court order; and justified disclosure in the public interest. It is also a defence if you can show that the controller would have consented had they known or if you had a reasonable (if incorrect) belief that you were authorised to disclose. This offence is similar to the one in the previous 1998 Data Protection Act – however it is extended to include the retention of personal data. As we discuss in the context of intellectual property in Chapter Eight (see under the paragraph headed "*The learned behaviours paradigm*"), there is a tendency of machine learning systems to retain what I have described as "*information residuals*" – principally the associative and correlative aspects describing statistical patterns and correlations in data used by the system (rather than the content of that data itself) – being retained by the machine learning system in an analogous fashion to a taught human being. The simple anthropomorphic analogy is that once something is learned, it cannot be unlearned. Clearly personal data processed by machine learning systems can be returned once it has been used – the question is whether what remains – the *information residuals* – constitutes retention for the purposes of this offence.

Re-identification of de-identified personal data

Section 171 creates an offence of re-identification of de-identified personal data: *"(1) It is an offence for a person knowingly or recklessly to re-identify information that is de-identified personal data without the consent*

[216] Section 170(1) of the Data Protection Act 2018

of the controller responsible for de-identifying the personal data. … (a) personal data is "de-identified" if it has been processed in such a manner that it can no longer be attributed, without more, to a specific data subject; (b) a person "re-identifies" information if the person takes steps which result in the information no longer being de-identified within the meaning of paragraph (a)"[217]. This offence is aimed at protecting data which has been *pseudonymised* (where re-identification is possible) (as opposed to fully anonymised where it should be impossible to re-identify data subjects). Users of machine learning systems should be mindful of the powerful ability of such systems to apply predictive analytics to the data that they process (see earlier in this chapter under the heading "*Predictive Analytics*"). In the context of our immediate debate the risk must be to prevent or at least put in place measures to avoid a machine learning system from *deriving* or *inferring* sufficient characteristics in the data it processes to inadvertently re-identify data subjects.

Open Data

Moving away from the UK's post-Brexit data legislation, it is worth now covering developments in Open Data.

It is an oft quoted fact that more data has been created by humans in the past two years than the entire previous history of the human race.[218] And yet we live and work in a fragmented data world with little or no consistency in the way data are shared as between individuals, enterprise and nation states.

"Open Data" initiatives are the response to this fragmentation. They are driven by the recognition that the removal of "data siloes" will benefit society generally by improving access to information (and all the associated benefits that will bring, such as increased transparency and

[217] Section 171(1) & (2) of the Data Protection Act 2018

[218] See for example *Big Data: 20 Mind-Boggling Facts Everyone Must Read*, Bernard Marr https://www.forbes.com/sites/bernardmarr/2015/09/30/big-data-20-mind-boggling-facts-everyone-must-read/?sh=3080bec717b1

accountability) and will accelerate progress and innovation in specific technologies such as artificial intelligence and machine learning, which themselves depend upon data.

Put simply, Open Data encompasses the initiatives that are taking place globally to share and improve access to data. In this part of the chapter we'll take a look at some of the steps that are being taken to facilitate open access to data.

The EU's Strategy for Data

The European Union has long taken the concept of Open Data seriously. Indeed, as far back as 2003 it enacted a measure referred to as the Public Sector Information or PSI Directive[219], which was ultimately replaced by the Open Data Directive[220]. The Open Data Directive focusses on the economic aspects of the re-use of public information as an EU-wide resource, rather than on access to information by European Citizens. It has now taken the concept of Open Data further, in part driven by the imperative of putting in place a complementary coherent strategy for artificial intelligence and machine learning technologies.

What the strategy aims to achieve is the facilitation of a "single market" for data, which should be able to flow freely within the EU and across different market sectors. One of the ways it proposes to achieve this is by the creation of common European "data spaces" in strategic sectors, such as industrial manufacturing, mobility, health, financial, agriculture, public administration and skills[221]. As the Commission itself states "*...This should lead to the availability of large pools of data in these sectors and domains, combined with the technical tools and infrastructures necessary*

219 Directive 2003/98

220 Directive 2019/1024

221 Ibid., page 22-23

to use and exchange data..."[222].

EU Data Governance Act

The Data Governance Act aims to improve data governance mechanisms and implement data sharing mechanisms across the EU by setting up common European "data spaces" in strategic domains in sectors such as health, environment, energy, agriculture, mobility, finance, manufacturing, public administration and skills. The Data Governance Act entered into force on 23rd June 2022 and will be applicable following a grace period from September 2023.

The EU Data Act

Following on from the Data Governance Act, the draft EU Data Act seeks sets down rules for data sharing across Europe. This measure is intended primarily to introduce a governance framework in relation to connected products, such as "*internet of things*" (or "IoT") products and other smart connected devices. As such it is likely to be relevant to AI applications (and providers) that utilise such devices. Amongst other rights, the Data Act introduces a right allowing consumers access to such connected data, as well as the ability to switch cloud providers.

On 27th June 2023, the EU Council and Commission reached a provisional agreement on harmonised rules supporting fair access to and use of data.

Data Trusts

The term "Data Trust" was first coined in a 2017 report[223] prepared by Dame Wendy Hall (professor of Computer Science at the University of Southampton) and Jérôme Pesenti (chief executive of BenevolentTech)

---

222 Ibid., page 21

223 *Growing the Artificial Intelligence Industry in the UK* – Otherwise known as the Hall-Pesenti Review

as part of a review into the UK's Artificial Intelligence industry.

Data Trusts were conceived as an approach to replicate the traditional characteristics and benefits of trusts to the stewardship and custody of data. The concept entails one party authorising another the "*data trustee*" to make decisions about data on their behalf, often for the benefit of a wider group of "*data beneficiaries*" or stakeholders. The idea follows that like a traditional trust, the data trustee would assume a fiduciary duty towards the ultimate data beneficiaries[224].

As at the date of writing, there is no legislation in the UK or elsewhere in the world to formalise the concept of data trusts, so the idea remains theoretical.

The UK's Open Data Institute however has provided examples of entities that operate in an analogous manner, such as the UK Biobank which was set up to steward genetic data and is constituted as a charitable company[225]. There are also moves in private enterprise to set up digitally framed data trusts. Sightline Innovation for example, a Canadian based business, has set up what it calls a trusted data collaboration platform which is designed to operate in much the same manner as a data trust, enabling interoperability whilst maintaining data compliance and governance[226].

Data Intermediaries

Aside from the data trust model, there are many other forms of what I have termed "data intermediary" that are positioning themselves as trusted data interchanges.

One of the key challenges in enabling a form of digitalised data exchange is the reality that aside from the fact that much data is held in fragmented

---

224 See What is a Data Trust: www. https://theodi.org/article/what-is-a-data-trust

225 Ibid.

226 See www.sightlineinnovation.com

silos, the format of the data itself is incompatible and does not lend itself to sharing. As such the market has turned to solutions that are attempting to provide a standardised data interchange format as a prelude to fully digitalised sharing.

One such business, EngineB[227] is focussed on just this task and is developing what it terms common data models for the flow of data between audit, legal and tax professionals and their clients. The theory is that by standardising the data used by law firms and accountancy practices, it will be much easier for clients to change their professional services advisors (this could conceivably be done by the flick of a proverbial switch). The other advantage is that audit businesses could simply monitor in real time the bank transactions of an audited business to evaluate against tax and other reporting governance rules, as well as apply all of the powerful benefits of data analytics discussed earlier in this chapter.

Data Commons

Finally, it is worth discussing the concept of Data Commons. This is a term which has been coined to refer to an open data licensing framework which is based upon similar principles to Open-Source Software licensing. A particular example of this approach is the one adopted by the Linux Foundation[228], which has developed a Community Data License Agreement[229]. The Linux Foundation CDLA is essentially split into two forms. The CLDA-Sharing[230] license embodies the principles of "copyleft"[231] in a data licence, in essence providing that downstream

227 See www.engineb.com

228 https://www.linuxfoundation.org/

229 https://cdla.dev/

230 https://cdla.dev/sharing-1-0/

231 Copyleft is the practice of granting the right to freely distribute and modify intellectual property with the requirement that the same rights be preserved in derivative works created from that property

recipients can use and modify that data (and are also required to share their changes to that data) and the CDLA-Permissive[232] license, which allows modification of data without any obligation to share such changes or modifications.

232 https://cdla.dev/permissive-1-0/

CHAPTER SEVEN

AUTOMATED FACIAL RECOGNITION

Automated facial recognition technologies (or "*AFR*") have recently garnered significant public attention and comment. Technological advances in artificial intelligence and machine learning have dramatically improved the utility of AFR which is increasingly being deployed in both commercial and state sponsored contexts.

Whilst it is true to say that the legal position in relation to Automated Facial Recognition is evolving, it is not correct to assume that there is no regulation.

AFR technology sits in a complex regulatory area which is a fusion of artificial intelligence, data processing, biometric data handling and surveillance, justifying a discussion in its own right.

By its nature, much of the existing law applicable to AFR is "use case" dependent and will apply differently, for example, if you are using the technology as part of an active video surveillance application, querying a pre-existing facial database, or a combination of both. In the European Union, as we have seen, the proposed new Artificial Intelligence Act now places strict restrictions on the extent to which facial recognition databases can be created and used, in particular by outlawing systems that create or expand such databases through large scale indiscriminate web-scraping from the internet or by CCTV footage[233], and by proscribing

[233] See Chapter Four for a more detailed discussion of the AIA and in particular Article 5 1 d b of the EU Parliament Text (Amendment 225)

the use of real time biometric identification in public spaces[234].

In the United States, some individual states now have legislation which (distinct from data protection related measures) make the collection of biometric data (which by its definition includes facial data) subject to strict consent requirements[235].

Different laws and codes of conduct will apply depending upon the extent to which a particular facial recognition application is used on public or private property and, of course, state actors such as the police, counter-terrorism and intelligence services will be bound by a separate regime applicable to the covert gathering and use of such data which is outside the scope of this chapter. Each use case will also likely fall under the oversight of a different, or multiple, regulators.

Misuse of AFR taps into wider public unease over the covert use and capturing of such biometric data and has the potential to cause serious reputational damage to a business (or state authority) if it fails to sensitively take into account the wider societal implications of use – let alone the narrower regulatory implications.

Recent studies have also indicated that the technology may not be as accurate as initially thought, an issue which was considered, in the case of *R (Bridges) v. Chief Constable of South Wales Police*[236], discussed further below. This makes any use case evaluation of AFR even more important.

---

234 See Article 5 1 d of the EU Parliament Text (Amendment 220)

235 The most prominent of these is the Biometric Information Privacy Act, or BIPA, in Illinois of 2008, see https://www.ilga.gov/legislation/ilcs/ilcs3.asp?ActID=3004&ChapterID=57

236 [2020] EWCA Civ 1058

Data Protection

Aside from regulatory constraints created by the Artificial Intelligence Act in the European Union (discussed at length in Chapter Five), so far as the UK is concerned, any analysis of the compliance of an AFR system will inevitably need to start with an assessment of its adherence to the data protection regime under the General Data Protection Regulation and Data Protection Act 2018 ("DPA 2018"), and relevant guidance issued by the Information Commissioner's Office ("ICO").

Facial images themselves are classed as personal data (i.e. data that can readily identify individuals) but processing by an AFR system, brings with it extra stringent regulation. As we discussed in Chapter Six, this is because biometric facial data used to *uniquely identify* an individual[237] is classified as "special category data", or sensitive data. The general principle here is that such data cannot be processed under the legitimate interests lawful processing ground: explicit consent needs to be relied upon instead. In addition to these considerations, it is likely that the AFR application will be relying on some form of automated processing, so considerations raised by Article 22 of the GDPR will also need to be factored in.

All of the above raises substantial conceptual issues about the extent to which it is actually feasible to implement the technology within the UK[238] as in many use cases of AFR, individuals are instantly recognised by such systems long before they have the opportunity to pro-actively consent to their facial data being processed. In a sense this is another manifestation of the structural difficulties that the GDPR has with artificial intelligence and machine learning that I have highlighted elsewhere in this book.

To take a particular example, in the United States, Amazon has been

---

[237] Article 9(1) GDPR

[238] In the EU the practice of using AFR in publicly accessible spaces will be explicitly prohibited under the AIA (see earlier Article 5 1 d of the EU Parliament Text)

rolling out a chain of stores branded "*Amazon Go*". These are physical stores which typically carry groceries. Shoppers simply enter and take goods from the shelves – there is no checkout process. Instead, that is handled by Amazon's facial recognition algorithms. Shoppers registered on Amazon's Go app are recognised by Amazon's systems as they enter the Go store, and their account is automatically debited when they leave with their selected items[239].

Applying that example to the UK, it would seem apparent that proactive consent could be obtained through the Amazon Go app, but what of shoppers who enter the store and are not registered with Amazon at all? The mere fact that the AFR system scans their face in an attempt to identify whether or not they are a registered customer puts the retailer into breach of its obligations under the GDPR as such people will not have been given the opportunity to decline to have their facial images scanned. This is of course before consideration is given to facial data which may be acquired from demographic groups that require even more special consideration under the GDPR, such as children, who may lack the capacity to provide effective consent.

Attempts to introduce the technology thus far in the UK have been limited to security-based applications, for what seem to be precisely these reasons. Facewatch[240], a UK business relies on the *substantial public interest* exception to the consent provisions of the UK Data Protection Act on the basis that it is justified in the public interest to prevent the commission of crime (in this case, shoplifting). This approach has yet to be substantively tested in the Courts[241].

Other substantive issues to be considered include ensuring that the

---

239 See *How 'Amazon Go' works: The technology behind the online retailer's groundbreaking new grocery store* https://www.geekwire.com/2016/amazon-go-works-technology-behind-online-retailers-groundbreaking-new-grocery-store/

240 www.facewatch.co.uk

241 Again, this type of AI use case is likely to be proscribed under the AIA regime in the European Union

application is designed with a view to maintaining privacy (referred to as "*privacy by design*"). It is also best practice in such circumstances to ensure that a comprehensive data protection impact assessment is carried out as such processing is likely to have a high degree of impact on affected individuals[242]. Indeed the UK's ICO has made it clear that this must be carried out by law enforcement when live facial recognition technology is used in public places[243]. As we discussed in prior Chapters, this requirement is now likely to be supplemented in the UK by AI related Impact Assessments.[244]

Understanding how AFR data will be held and processed is vital to determining legality.

Human Rights

Turning to Human Rights, Article 8 of the European Convention of Human Rights ("ECHR") provides for a right to respect for one's private and family life, home and correspondence and is directly actionable under English law through the mechanism of the Human Rights Act 1998. The right is clearly designed to circumscribe and limit intrusive activity which could damage privacy. Although clearly applicable to "state sponsored" uses, it is wise to consider these principles in a private sector context and to consider how an AFR application might interfere with those rights in such situations.

Current police trials of AFR have been subject to challenge by human

[242] See Article 35(3) of the GDPR which requires a DPIA when there are "systematic and extensive evaluation of personal aspects based on automated processing, including profiling, on which decisions are made that produce legal or similarly significant effects; large-scale processing of special categories of personal data; or systematic monitoring of publicly-accessible areas on a large scale"

[243] See Information Commissioner's Opinion: The use of live facial recognition technology by law enforcement in public places, 31 October 2019 Reference: 2019/01 https://ico.org.uk/media/about-the-ico/documents/2616184/live-frt-law-enforcement-opinion-20191031.pdf

[244] See Chapter Fourteen for a discussion on the UK's AI Governance White Paper

rights organisations on this basis (as we discuss shortly in the context of the *South Wales Police* case).

Protection of Freedoms Act

Chapter 2 of Part 1 of the Protection of Freedoms Act 2012 ("PFA 2012")[245] provides for oversight by the Biometrics Commissioner of certain biometric data gathered under the Police and Criminal Evidence Act 1998 – principally fingerprints, DNA samples and custody pictures but increasingly also facial databases (such as the National Police Database) maintained by law enforcement authorities. Chapter 1 of Part 2 (s33) of the PFA 2012 governs the use and regulation of CCTV and other surveillance camera technology by "relevant authorities" (principally state actors), and provides for the Surveillance Camera Commissioner, of which more below.

Surveillance Camera Code of Practice

The Surveillance Camera Code of Practice 2021[246] ("SCC Code") applies to the use of "overt" video surveillance systems in public places by relevant public authorities, where compliance is mandatory. Principle 12 specifically refers to the use and/or processing of images obtained by CCTV for purposes such as facial recognition. The code is administered by the Surveillance Camera Commissioner ("SCC").

Where AFR is used as part of a public authority administered public scheme, the SCC will have jurisdiction and can enforce compliance with the SCC Code. The SCC's mission is to ensure voluntary compliance with the SCC Code by unregulated (private) entities, so although not directly applicable in such circumstances, it is still a factor that needs to

245 https://www.legislation.gov.uk/ukpga/2012/9/contents/enacted

246 The original 2013 Code of Practice was updated in 2021 to take account of new legislation and also the impact of the Bridges case discussed later in this chapter – see https://assets.publishing.service.gov.uk/government/uploads/system/uploads/attachment_data/file/1035067/Surveillance_Camera_CoP_Accessible_PDF.pdf

be considered.

Equality Act

If the use of AFR could produce biased outcomes (in particular through facial training data that does not adequately represent the ethnic diversity of modern society) then it pays also to be mindful of the impact of the Equality Act 2010[247] ("EA 2010") and in particular the need to avoid both direct and indirect discrimination. Again, these are concepts which are discussed more substantively in Chapter Nine on Bias and Discrimination. This particular aspect of AFR system use was discussed at length in the *South Wales Police* case, see later in this chapter.

Private Security Industry Act

Finally, the use of AFR which involves a security application extending to public spaces and which includes CCTV monitoring and/or door supervision, may constitute a licensable activity under the Private Security Industry Act 2001[248].

This legislation was originally enacted to provide a licensing regime for the private security industry which had suffered from a poor reputation previously. Licences are administered by the Security Industry Association ("SIA"). Failure to obtain a licence, when one is needed, is a criminal offence which may be punishable by fines and/or imprisonment.

Facial recognition decisions

So that was a very high level view of the relevant legislative framework applying to commercial use cases. What then of the applicable case law? As at the date of writing, there are several domestic and international facial recognition cases and enforcement actions worth discussing.

---

247 https://www.legislation.gov.uk/ukpga/2010/15/contents

248 https://www.legislation.gov.uk/ukpga/2001/12/contents

R (Bridges) v. Chief Constable of South Wales Police

The South Wales Police case is a UK Court of Appeals case which was concluded in August 2020. The case itself is interesting as an insight into the thinking of the UK Court of Appeals although the principles arising from it in relation to AFR are necessarily limited to use by public sector organisations and therefore will be of limited application to private sector use.

In this case, the South Wales Police ("SWP") were using an AFR pilot in Swansea city centre to match a "watchlist" of felons, suspects and other persons of interest to their facial database. Crucially for the purpose of their analysis, the police immediately deleted facial data in respect of unknown people and only retained data relating to facial matches. The plaintiff, Ed Bridges, had brought an appeal against an earlier Divisional Court judgment on a number of grounds challenging the lawfulness of SWP's use of the technology as a person in the vicinity of the SWP's AFR vans when in use.

The Court of Appeal agreed with the Divisional Court judgment which held that there had been interference with the appellant's Human Rights – specifically Article 8 of the ECHR, however crucially they disagreed with the lower court's assessment that the underlying law was sufficient to justify its use within Article 8(2). As the Data Protection Impact Assessment prepared by the SWP under s64 of the DPA 2018 had incorrectly concluded that there was no infringement of Article 8, the court found in consequence that it had failed to properly address the risks arising from the use of the AFR system.

At the core of the judgment were concerns that this insufficiency in law inadequately dealt with what the Court termed the "*who*" question (ie who should be identified as a "person of interest" on the SWP watchlist) and the "*where*" question (ie where deployment of AFR would be justified). Currently too much discretion was accorded to individual police officers in determining these issues (indeed the court referred to the discretion here as "*impermissibly wide*"). In terms of the existing legal framework the Court's view was that whilst the DPA 2018 formed an important part of the framework it was not sufficient by itself, and whilst the SCC Code briefly mentioned AFR, it did not deal specifically with these fundamental "*who*" and "*where*" issues.

Finally, and perhaps most controversially for the use of AFR in public sector contexts, the court held that in its use of the technology the SWP had not met its Public Sector Equality Duty (or "*PSED*"), in accordance with s149(1) of the EA 2010. The PSED is designed amongst other things to ensure that public sector authorities eliminate discrimination, harrassment, victimisation and any other conduct prohibited by the EA 2010. In sharp contradiction to the earlier Divisional Court judgment, the Court of Appeal held that SWP had failed the standard of the PSED by not investigating (or even considering) the potential for the AFR system to produce biased outcomes in relation to BAME community members.

There were many issues which were frustratingly not dealt with in a conclusive manner by the South Wales Police judgment. It is also apparent that the court's assessment of the insufficiency of the legal framework supporting public sector use of AFR will very likely lead to further legislative and policy interventions.

Skellefteå School Board

The Skellefteå School Board case[249] was a decision of the Swedish Data Protection Authority, Datainspektionen, a year ealier than *South Wales Police*, in August 2019.

In this case it was subsequently discovered that Anderstorps upper secondary school in the Swedish municipality of Skellefteå had been using facial recognition technology in a trial to log school students for attendance purposes. The pilot use of the technology had also been

[249] Not reported in English, but see https://www.imy.se/nyheter/2019/sanktionsavgift-for-ansiktsigenkanning-i-skola/ for the Swedish language transcript

implemented in an attempt to speed up and automate the daily registration process. Biometric data from students was captured in the form of photographs and associated with their full names. Consent had been obtained from the parents and/or legal guardians of the children concerned.

Ultimately the School was fined SEK 200,000 (around £17,000). The Swedish DPA found that an inadequate form of risk assessment had been carried out with no data protection impact assessment had been carried out and that contrary to Article 35 there was no formal data protection impact assessment. In addition it found that the processing of the children's biometric data was intrusive, and disproportionate, and could have been achieved in a less intrusive manner, contrary to Article 5 of the GDPR.

On the issue of consent, Datainspektionen found that notwithstanding that such had been obtained from parents and guardians, this could not be relied upon as there was an inequality of relationship between the Children and the School Board (such that any consent would have been brought into doubt).

Everalbum

In the United States the FTC[250] recently reached a settlement with a Calfornia-based developer of a photo app that it alleged had deceived consumers about the use of facial recognition technology[251], namely by not obtaining their consent to the acquistion of their biometric AFR data and also retaining it in circumstances where consumers had requested account deletion, in direct contravention of assurances made that such

250 Federal Trade Commission

251 See *California Company Settles FTC Allegations It Deceived Consumers about use of Facial Recognition in Photo Storage App* 11th January 2021, https://www.ftc.gov/news-events/press-releases/2021/01/california-company-settles-ftc-allegations-it-deceived-consumers

data would be deleted.

The settlement mandated that Everalbum, Inc. should obtain consumers express consent before using AFR on their photos and videos. What was also very notable was that the FTC mandated the a very wide deletion sanction: not just removal of the AFR data itself, but also the deletion of models and algorithms trained on the illegally applied AFR technology.

All of this does mean that applying AFR in both the public and private sectors remains a complex, evolving and delicate exercise wherever it is used. The utility of the technology needs to be balanced with thorny and substantial issues involving individual liberty and personal privacy.

Clearview AI

Nowhere is this dichotomy better illustrated than by reference to the case of Clearview AI.

Clearview AI is a US based AI company set up in 2017 to provide facial recognition technology, initially to companies and individuals but principally now to law enforcement entities around the world.

The company's facial image database is said to comprise at least 50 billion images of individuals which were scraped from publicly available internet sources, including major social media applications, ostensibly, and controversially, without any form of consent ever being obtained. The company operated without significant publicity until a New York Times article was published in 2020[252], describing its information gathering processes, and the nature of its facial recognition solution.

This led to a number of international cases challenging the legality of Clearview AI's business model:

[252] "The Secretive Company That Might End Privacy as We Know It", New York Times, January 2020, see https://www.nytimes.com/2020/01/18/technology/clearview-privacy-facial-recognition.html

United States

In the US, Clearview AI became the subject of class action law suits across a number of states, including Illinois, California, Virginia and New York. Most notably, a class action law suit was brought against it under Illinois' Biometric Information Privacy Act (BIPA) by the ACLU which was ultimately settled by Clearview AI. The terms of the settlement included permanently banned it from providing paid or free access to its facial recognition database to private entities nationwide across the US[253].

The European Union

Clearview's facial recognition offering has been deemed unlawful in a number of European member states: France's data protection regulator, the CNIL, issued a 20 million euro fine on 20th October 2022 for breaching the GDPR[254]. This followed a similar fine from the Greek data protection authority on 20th July 2022[255], and the Italian regulator, the Garante on 10th March 2022[256]. Austria's data protection regulator ruled Clearview AI's activities as unlawful but did not impose a fine[257]

As we have seen in discussions in Chapter Five and this chapter, new measures in the Artificial Intelligence Act designed to proscribe indiscriminate large scale web scraping in the context of obtaining

253 See: https://www.aclu.org/press-releases/big-win-settlement-ensures-clearview-ai-complies-with-groundbreaking-illinois

254 Articles 6 (Lawfulness of Processing), 12 (Transparency), 15 (Right of access by data subject), 17 (Right to be forgotten) and 31 (Co-operation with supervisory authority) of the GDPR were cited in the decision: see https://edpb.europa.eu/news/national-news/2023/facial-recognition-french-sa-imposes-penalty-payment-clearview-ai_en

255 See https://edpb.europa.eu/news/national-news/2022/hellenic-dpa-fines-clearview-ai-20-million-euros_en

256 See https://edpb.europa.eu/news/national-news/2022/facial-recognition-italian-sa-fines-clearview-ai-eur-20-million_en

257 See https://edpb.europa.eu/news/national-news/2023/decision-austrian-sa-against-clearview-ai-infringements-articles-5-6-9-27_en

training data for AI systems is largely a response to this case.

The UK

In May 2022, Clearview AI was fined £7.5 million for breaches of the UK GDPR and ordered by way of enforcement notice to stop processing the personal data of UK citizens, and delete any data on their systems relating to UK citizens[258].

Australia

In November 2021, the Office of the Australian Information Commissioner ruled that Clearview AI had breached the Australian Privacy Act 1988 and consequently the privacy of Australian citizens. It was effectively ordered to destroy existing Australian sourced images and to withdraw from the Australian market. It was also ordered to cease collecting facial images and biometrics from Australians[259].

---

258 See https://ico.org.uk/about-the-ico/media-centre/news-and-blogs/2022/05/ico-fines-facial-recognition-database-company-clearview-ai-inc/

259 See https://www.oaic.gov.au/newsroom/clearview-ai-breached-australians-privacy

CHAPTER EIGHT

INTELLECTUAL PROPERTY RIGHTS IN AI SYSTEMS

Traditionally intellectual property (or "*IP*") concepts form part of our established methods of protection for new technologies. In this chapter, we'll take a look at how IP can and cannot be used to protect investment and innovation in the development of artificial intelligence. We'll also consider whether intellectual property conventions, as in the context of causation earlier, may be breaking down, or at least fraying at the edges.

Before we examine some of the IP frameworks which might be applicable to machine learning, it is worthwhile taking some time to assess where the perceived *inherent value* in such technology lies, because in simple terms, if we can defend the valuable elements, we are more effectively protecting our entire AI asset. These considerations are clearly not only important from the perspective of the users and licensors of such technology, but also those who wish to obtain such systems through corporate activity (such as mergers and acquisitions).

As we learned in Chapter One, AI systems are not radically different from traditional computer systems in that they are essentially composed of two elements – the software which embodies the relevant AI model, and the computational hardware upon which it sits. Of course computational systems that host complex deep learning AI models are very sophisticated and can access huge amounts of processing power as well as harnessing petabytes of data – but they are still computers in the conventional sense.

At a superficial level one might say therefore that nothing has changed from an IP perspective, and that these are trite and settled issues: the computational hardware per se or in combination with software might in theory be eligible for patent protection under the Patents Act 1977, but that would require the elements of that Act to be made out – principally the element of industrial application[260] which requires a physical device or apparatus together with newness and an *inventive step* taking the physical device beyond the published *state of the art*[261].

Patents

Inventors of AI systems typically face real difficulties when looking to the Patents regime for legal protection. The first is that in many jurisdictions, including the UK and EU *disembodied software* is explicitly excluded from the scope of patent protection.

Then you have the problem of abstraction – in essence related to the problem of disembodied software – which is that if something is too abstract or can only be carried out in the human mind or as explained by the US patent office by a human being "*with pen and paper*", then it is not capable of protection. The European Patent office refers this as a scheme or rules and methods for performing mental acts. Finally, mathematical methods, such as algorithms per se are also excluded from scope.

You can see therefore that there are some quite considerable conceptual difficulties in getting a patent in relation to something which is potentially software related and highly abstract.

Despite these difficulties, machine learning patents are growing internationally at quite a phenomenal rate. Lots of efforts are expended as the 20-year monopoly period granted over patented technology is an extremely valuable right to have.

So how are potential patent owners getting around these difficulties? Well, the first point to make in this regard is that entities with deep pockets will sometimes take a "*brute force*" approach – that is to say they

---

260 See s1(1)(c) Patents Act 1977

261 See s1(1)(b) Patents Act 1977

will deluge the relevant patent office with so many applications that ultimately some will be granted. This is perhaps oversimplifying the position however: a granted patent is not necessarily a valid patent – only a court can uphold validity after a patent challenge.

The European Patent Office (EPO) and US Patent and Trademark office (USPTO) each have their own attitude, policy and approach in relation to patent examination and registration. Any successful application will obviously need to conform to this. Historically the view has always been that it is anecdotally easier to have your software related invention patented in the United States – but current trends do not necessarily reflect this, with the EPO certainly becoming more receptive to applied AI use cases.

The most important barrier to break through is of course making sure that your invention is not classified as "*software*". This is where the concept of the "*Computer Implemented Invention*" or CII has arisen. In essence this is a term which has been developed on a semantic sense to avoid the use of "*software*" in patents.

Merely referring to CII in an application is not sufficient however – the proposed invention needs to critically have a "*technical effect*". What this means in very simple and general terms is that the system needs to manifest in a way that goes beyond the abstract – or at least be expressed in the application as having a technical effect which goes beyond the purely abstract. A simple example might be something that uses machine learning to actuate a robot limb or generate synthetic speech. Obviously this is not a binary analysis – so there are likely to be areas which are highly abstract but which do get granted patent protection, merely through the manner in which they are expressed.

We must not forget as well that for a patent to be successful, an invention also needs to be novel – that is to say beyond the current *state of the art*. Obviously there is a tension to be drawn here around explaining the proposed invention in detail, including the state of the "*prior art*" and the pitfall of a really great explanation which is so good that it could lead a patent examiner into the fallacy that the invention is in fact obvious!

One of the biggest potential issues in relation to the patenting of "black box" machine learning solutions has to be that of *sufficiency*. If you cannot explain technically how it works, then in order to satisfy the disclosure requirements for a patent (which are that someone unfamiliar with its operation needs to understand how it works) then it may be that you have to disclose the underlying datasets which are used to train it as part of the application.

The final point to note is that several EPO examiners have indicated that using pseudocode and/or UML[262] in an AI patent application – that is to say modelling structures derived from either coding or diagrams, is often far more useful and revealing (particularly in terms of defining the algorithmic "technical effect") than normal language[263].

FRAND Licensing models?

With an increasingly crowded field of registered patents – how free actually are you to create new technologies? This is an increasing concern for the AI industry which is now dominating global patent registrations[264].

The AI market is relatively new and has yet to evolve consistent approaches, however one suggestion has been that it should follow the lead of more mature technological industries and adopt a telecoms style approach which allows for patent pools and FRAND licensing (so called

262 Unified Modeling Language

263 *How to Help an EPO Examiner and Improve Your Odds of Patenting a Computer-Implemented Invention* Gene Quinn, July 21, 2019 – see https://www.ipwatchdog.com/2019/07/21/epo-examiner-patenting-computer-implemented-inventions/id=111061/

264 A WIPO report published in 2019 (Technology Trends) indicated that Machine Learning is the dominant AI technique and is included now in more than one third of *all* identified inventions

fair, reasonable and non-discriminatory terms).

This type of licensing permits the sharing of complementary patents to develop complex technology (an approach which is adopted in the telecommunications industry for example), and has the societal benefit of improving compatibility for consumers (a particular example in the mobile telecoms space is network interoperability as between the manufacturers of different handsets).

The Machine as inventor

As we'll see in a moment in relation to Copyright, there is specific provision in the UK Copyright, Designs and Patents Act 1988 (the "CDPA") for the creation of computer-generated copyright works – somewhat of a departure from other jurisdictions, such as the United States[265]. What then of the position under Patent law where it is claimed that that the author of an invention is in fact a machine (or that the invention has been created by artificial intelligence?)

This was in fact the position which was alleged in the long running *DABUS* patent cases which were considered by the US, UK and European Patent Offices.

The basic premise of DABUS[266] was that artificial intelligence cannot, at least under current patent laws, be considered to be an inventor. DABUS, itself a creation of a human inventor, Stephen Thaler, was alleged to have independently devised two separate inventions, one which was described as beverage container, the other as a fractal light signal for attracting

265 See for example, and by analogy, the US case of ***Naruto (PETA) vs. Slater*** 888 F. 3d 418 (9th Cir. 2018), the so called "monkey selfie" case. PETA (People for the Ethical Treatment of Animals) filed a claim against a photographer, David Slater, on the basis that a selfie photograph taken allegedly by Naruto, a macaque monkey was not in fact the property of Slater but was owned by the monkey itself. The US 9th Circuit Court of Appeals ruled that copyright under the US Copyright Act 1976, 17 U.S.C. §§ 101-1332 could not vest in an animal

266 *'device for the autonomous bootstrapping of unified sentience'*

attention. Mr Thaler named DABUS itself as the inventor in the applications which were filed at the respective patent offices. In each case it was essentially determined that an inventor had to be a natural human being[267]. In the UK the decision of the IPO was subsequently affirmed by the High Court[268].

It seems for the moment at least, that this avenue is closed for patent registration: not a surprise when one considers that the wider debate around machine personality has likewise been shut down. It does however create wider uncertainty about the ability of enterprise to invest in the use of AI when creating patentable IP. This is because a failure to list the correct inventor can open such patents up to challenge and ultimately render them unenforceable.

Copyright

Subject to the above considerations, disembodied software does not (at least within the EU and UK) qualify for patent protection[269] – here we must look to the CDPA which specifically calls out human and machine generated software as capable of protection by copyright[270] provided it meets the required standards of originality. However, it is here that we see some of the logic underpinning software as copyrightable works

267 USPTO Decision: In re Application of Application No.: 16/524,350: https://www.uspto.gov/sites/default/files/documents/16524350_22apr2020_3.pdf; EPO Decision: https://www.epo.org/news-events/news/2020/20200128.html; UK IPO Decision: https://www.ipo.gov.uk/p-challenge-decision-results/o74119.pdf

268 [2020] WLD(D)526 see: https://www.bailii.org/ew/cases/EWHC/Patents/2020/2412.html

269 s1(2)(c) Patents Act 1977 excludes specifically "a scheme, rule or method for performing a mental act, playing a game or doing business, or a program for a computer"

270 s3(1)(b) Copyright, Designs and Patents Act 1977 specifically includes computer programs as literary works and s12(7) makes explicit provision for works that are generated by Computer, reducing the applicable copyright term to 50 years from the end of the calendar year in which the work was created

beginning to break down.

Whilst the CDPA does make provision for computer generated works to be protected by Copyright[271], this still presumes a causal connection (albeit vague) between the relevant acts of the computer and human preparatory work – section 9(3) provides that "*In the case of a literary, dramatic, musical or artistic work which is computer-generated, the author shall be taken to be the person by whom the arrangements necessary for the creation of the work are undertaken.*". The term "*Computer generated*" is defined as follows "*in relation to a work, means that the work is generated by computer in circumstances such that there is no human author of the work.*"[272]. As we have seen, and as I explain further below, machine learning models are increasingly abstracted from human intervention and inherently opaque, and thus, it is argued, the causal connection implied by section 9(3) is becoming increasingly redundant. Indeed the one UK case that has to date been decided in relation to computer generated works – *Nova Productions ltd v. Mazooma Games*[273] applying section 9(3) of the CDPA, provides a highly problematic outcome for the "*learned behaviours*" paradigm I discuss below. Mazooma held that a series of computer-generated video game "frames" were either authored directly by the machine or by the person providing arrangements necessary for the creation of the work – in this case, the programmer – and not the *player* of the game. In our current debate, is it not the *trainer* of the machine learning system which is most analogous to the *player*?

As we discovered in Chapter One, the key elements forming a machine learning system are the ***Model***, the ***Parameters*** and the ***Learner*** which together form the Artificial Neural Network.

The CDPA provides that a literary work "*means any work, other than a dramatic or musical work, which is written, spoken or sung, and accordingly*

[271] s9(3) Copyright, Designs and Patents Act 1988

[272] s178 Copyright, Designs and Patents Act 1988

[273] [2007] EWCA Civ 219, [2007] Bus LR 1032

includes...(b) a computer program" and "*(c) preparatory design material for a computer program*"[274]. It would seem evident in this context that at least the AI ***Model*** (the logical framework within which the system operates) described above will potentially be eligible for copyright protection. Whilst the CDPA provides no guidance as to originality required for such protection, recital eight of the 2009 Software Directive[275] provides that in determining whether "*a computer program is an original work, no tests as to the qualitative or aesthetic merits of the program should be applied.*" This is to be read in conjunction with Article 1 which provides that "*a computer program shall be protected if it is original in the sense that it is the author's own intellectual creation. No other criteria shall be applied to determine its eligibility for protection.*"[276]. Clearly the framers of the Directive intended copyright protection to extend merely to the coding aspects of the software concerned and in turn expressly excluded the *outputs* or *products* of that code. Whilst there is no such guidance in the UK CDPA, the Directive (as an element of post Brexit retained EU law) should be considered as influential on the approach taken by courts and tribunals within the UK.

Obviously at the time the relevant Copyright legislation was framed, software (whether machine or human created) consisted of rigidly programmed linear instruction sets that had no (or at least very limited) ability to adapt and "learn" according to data inputs: the exponential rise in use and development of artificial intelligence has occurred relatively recently.

As we have seen, machine learning systems lack a direct correlation between human input and machine generated output – their models are created within the framework of software but as they are trained or exposed to sufficient amounts of data, their outputs adapt (they are modified by the *Learner* element we discussed in Chapter One, above),

[274] s(3)(1) of the Copyright, Designs and Patents Act 1977

[275] Directive 2009/24/EC on the legal protection of computer programs

[276] See Article 1(3), Directive 2009/24/EC

and thus they become more adept at solving the application that they are presented with. Machine learning trainers are therefore in a highly influential position to tune and direct system outputs (in this regard I direct the reader back to comments made in relation to the *Mazooma* case).

It is this complex mass of tuned, biased and weighted variables applied progressively to the machine learning model during the training process – in more anthropomorphic terms – "*learned*" or "*trained*" behaviour (discussed further below) – which provides the key difference and arguably the demonstrable and substantial *value* to the users of AI systems. Other than this distinguishing feature there is no underlying difference in the technological hardware and processing platform as between trained and untrained systems. Of course, continuing the anthropomorphic analogy, which is entirely apposite here, the other aspect of learned behaviours is that once they are learned, they cannot be unlearned, and the more relevant learning and experience you are exposed to, the better you get at solving a particular problem. This is of particular importance in relation to the large data sets that AI systems are exposed to, especially in circumstances where such data sets are *licensed* for use (implying some form of return of the material so licensed) rather than assigned permanently or owned by the user. We'll consider these two elements of what I have termed the *learned behaviours paradigm* in a moment.

Separately, and distinct from the system itself, there is clearly value in the training data sets that are provided to the relevant machine learning system. This is akin of course to the training materials provided to a child in school education – feed it the right information and hopefully the right outputs will emerge (the child will be properly educated). Don't feed it at all, or feed it the wrong information and what you'll get out of it will also be a waste of time – as the saying goes, "*garbage in, garbage out*". Curating and assembling training data sets (whether on a supervised or unsupervised basis) is, as we have already mentioned, a critical part in the evolution and development of a useful artificially intelligent system. One has to assume that there will therefore be some not inconsiderable level of skill involved in creating such data sets, and calibrating them to ensure maximal value from a machine learning system.

Algorithms

Algorithms sit at the heart of artificially intelligent systems – clearly the efficiency or otherwise of such algorithms drives the usefulness of such systems – however it is important to note that algorithms *per se* are nothing more than a complex procedural expression or set of rules – a formula.

In the case of machine learning systems, it is algorithms which define at the most fundamental level how the system handles and manages the data inputted into it.

Algorithms fall within a grey area in intellectual property law. When they are expressed as pure mathematical formulae, they are unlikely to be capable of copyright protection as they represent an expression of mathematical fact. However when expressed, encoded and articulated as part of software, they are more likely in principle to enjoy copyright protection.

So far as patent law is concerned, obviously an algorithm represents an idea or concept. As such, the general discussion above on patentability applies. Unless the prior considerations we discussed are followed, they are unlikely to be patentable *per se*. In any event, focussing merely on the protection of the learning or activation algorithms used by an artificially intelligent system (if indeed such are capable of intellectual property protection) solves only one part of the IP jigsaw. An algorithm to a machine learning system is an expression of its most fundamental functions – taking such an approach to the exclusion of the other elements listed in this chapter would be much like attempting to protect the representative chemical synaptic functions of neurons in a human brain whilst excluding its thoughts.

The "learned behaviours" paradigm

Earlier on in this chapter, we described how artificial intelligence systems develop useful learned behaviours over the course of their training process by the refinement of weights, biases and variables within their AI *models* (whether on a supervised, unsupervised or reinforcement basis) and how more comprehensively or effectively trained systems are demonstrably more valuable than their counterparts which although technologically equivalent, have not undergone this process. It is worth recapping the concept of machine learning in order to get a clear picture of what is actually happening inside a machine learning system.

As we saw in Chapter One, what a neural network does when it "*learns*" is apply a series of weights and biases across the successive artificial neuron layers in its network to influence activations within those individual neurons and ultimately the output layer, hopefully achieving the desired correct output. It is ultimately a mathematical process of refinement but a process which leads to optimised and useful output. As noted above, I refer to this for reasons of conceptual ease as "learned behaviour".

We also considered that exposure to training or calibrating sets of data during this training process (and indeed to live production data during normal operational use) could lead to some elements of the data set – principally the associative aspects describing statistical patterns and correlations rather than the content itself – being retained by the machine learning system in an analogous fashion to a taught human being. How then should this paradigm be managed by intellectual property law?

We have seen that copyright will somewhat imperfectly protect the software model or framework within which an artificial intelligence system sits. On the same basis, it might also protect relevant machine learning algorithms but only if they are expressed in a software form. It cannot (in its current guise) protect the output or *learned behaviours* of that system, unless they are expressed in an immutable form in the software construct of the ***Model*** (as discussed earlier). Immutability however is typically not a characteristic of learned behaviours. As with a human, as a machine learning system is trained and exposed to more data, it becomes better at its assigned task – or in more mechanistic terms, the output becomes further optimised.

Knowhow

Traditionally "*know how*", that is to say the knowledge and knowhow gained by a person experientially and locked up in their heads, is not something that is capable of intellectual property protection. Typically this is because, in human terms, intellectual property protects the *expressions* of ideas rather than the idea itself. Without delving too deeply into the realms of the philosophical, can it be said that the "knowhow" generated by artificially intelligent systems is equivalent?

In practical terms of course, machine learning systems are created by human beings and (for the moment at least) do not share an equivalence with us. They are undoubtedly complex, and we as humans have difficulty understanding on a practical (and even theoretical level) how such systems reach their decisions, but they are still a construct of human endeavour.

Whilst copyright and patent law are unlikely to be of much use in relation to protecting the learned behaviours of trained artificially intelligent systems, it is submitted that in this context there is one intellectual property route that might be extended to protect them, and that is the *trade secret.*

A trade secret is typically a commercially valuable process or item of know-how which has been kept from the public domain.

Traditionally the UK has not had a trade secret regime but has relied on the concept of breach of confidence for protection of such items. Whilst this common law regime provides much equivalence with Trade Secret law, it has traditionally suffered from some conceptual difficulties with the concept of industrial espionage. The United States has long had a trade secret law – see for example the Uniform Trade Secrets Act of 1979 and in this context the EU is perceived as having lagged behind in its intellectual property regime. This ultimately led to the *Directive on the Protection of undisclosed know-how and business information (trade secrets)*[277] or Trade Secrets Directive. The Trade Secrets Directive provides that an item of intellectual property will qualify for protection if: it "*(a) it is secret in the sense that it is not, as a body or in the precise configuration and assembly of its components, generally known among or readily accessible to persons within the circles that normally deal with the kind of information in question; (b) it has commercial value because it is secret; (c) it has been subject to reasonable steps under the circumstances, by the person lawfully in control of the information, to keep it secret*".[278] In the context of our current debate, the learned behaviours (or optimised outputs) of an artificially intelligent system are likely to have been developed through a careful process which will be a combination of training, tuning and exposure to carefully selected training data sets (of which more later). Much of this process is likely to have been developed through experimentation, trial and error and of course considerable investment.

It is likely in the circumstances that the "optimised" machine learning system that results will result in competitive advantage for its owner, and such owner is unlikely to want to voluntarily throw that competitive advantage away by disclosing it to competitors.

Provided the owner has exercised reasonable precautions to keep the process described above away from the public domain, it is plausible that they should be able to claim trade secret protection under the regime proposed by the Trade Secrets Directive. The foregoing should of course be tempered by the fact that there is a very active community that will be driven by "*open access*" principles to information for the greater good of advancing research into artificial intelligence and there are equally speaking very many open-source derived AI algorithms and approaches

[277] Directive (EU) 2016/943

[278] Trade Secrets Directive Article 1(a),(b) & (c)

which obviously will be unlikely to qualify for such intellectual property protection.

Data sets

Custom assembled training data sets (or indeed operational data sets that have been assembled for processing by an AI system) are also, for the reasons articulated above, likely to qualify for similar trade secret style protection.

The informed reader may also wonder about the reach of the Database Directive[279] into this domain – however as that directive is intended to cover a "*scheme of arrangement of data*" (ie a systemically organised database[280]) it is unlikely to be of use in relation to most AI systems whose very power and flexibility comes from their ability to ingest and process multiple items of raw, heterogenous data from different and disparate data sources (sometimes referred to as "data lakes"). Although there are likely to be qualitative decisions made about the types and classes of data to be used for training machine learning systems it is improbable that such data sets would reach the levels of organisation equivalent to a classically ordered database. In the context of neural networks, there may be a role for the Database Directive tangentially in relation to the collective *weights* and *biases* which are applied to individual input neurons in order to influence the network's output (see our earlier discussion on this in the context of Chapter One) – however that analysis appears marginal when one considers that it depends upon these variables being able to be systematically extracted from the operation of the system itself in a useful and repeatable manner.

The second part of the learned behaviours paradigm we discussed above

---

279 96/9/EC implemented by the Copyright and Rights in Databases Regulations 1997

280 Article 1(2) of the Database Directive 96/9/EC provides that "database" means " a collection of independent works, data or other materials arranged in a systematic or methodical way and individually accessible by electronic or other means"

was the potential for an AI system to retain associative and relational elements of the data processed by it as part of the training or learning process – such retention enabling improvement in the system's ability to achieve its assigned tasks or in alternate terms, improving its skill level. Conceptually this is difficult to reconcile with traditional intellectual licensing models and data protection law which require the return or destruction of licensed materials at the end of the applicable licensing term or period of use. Irrespective of whether technically such is feasible, as a developer or owner of a machine learning system you are unlikely to want to hand back those associative or relational data elements (so called "*information residuals*") which have improved performance in your system. What this means in practical terms is that any licensing model must take account of these characteristics and either provide for a perpetual license of those data elements which are retained or a full assignment. A failure to do so may render the licensee potentially subject to an action for breach of contract.

Whether this proves to be a substantive issue in the future remains to be seen – practically speaking this is the way in which AI systems function so it would seem to be futile attempting to legislate otherwise. As a practitioner however, you should be aware of this pitfall and provide for appropriate carve outs in any third-party deals which are licensing data sets for machine learning systems.

Infringing and Derivative works

The final part of this chapter is really to flag the ongoing potential for machine learning systems to create infringing and derivative versions of copyrighted works. This is not of itself a new problem – new technologies have enabled a technologically sophisticated environment which empowers the YouTube generation to manipulate video and audio on domestic computers which has in turn driven a culture of plagiarism and derivative works – a perennial problem for major copyright holders. What is new however, and potentially disturbing, is the level of sophistication that AI provides to these users.

"*DeepFake*" software, which is now freely available to computer enthusiasts, enables facial substitution technology in video. Inevitably, this has been driven to the lowest common denominator which has involved pasting the faces of Hollywood "A" list actors into hard core pornography (a course of conduct that could of course give rise to wider defamatory issues) – however it doesn't take much imagination to see this technology being used by fans to paste themselves into their favourite franchises, to substitute or swap preferred actors in movies or even to resurrect long dead actors (something that Hollywood is beginning to dabble in on an "official" basis). Perhaps even more disturbingly given the recent trend of fake news, there are signs that this technology may be used to fake incendiary statements by politicians to fan the flames of extremism and to undermine democratic societies. Indeed California has been at the forefront of attempting to outlaw this use, and passed a State law in October 2019 making such use illegal[281]. This trend continues with the Artificial Intelligence Act currently being finalised by the European Union[282]. The AIA now requires that deep fake content is declared as such, and places obligations on the producers of AI systems to ensure that when using generative AI systems, such systems do not generate outputs in breach of subsisting EU law.

As I explained in Chapter Three, Generative AI systems have taken this debate to fiercely fought levels – pitting creative rights holders against AI developers. The issue here of course is the extent to which massive web scraping activity undertaken by companies such as OpenAI and Stability AI in training their models can be restricted from an intellectual property perspective[283]. As I mentioned in Chapter Three, these are issues which

---

281 See AB730 Deceptive Audio or Visual Media http://leginfo.legislature.ca.gov/faces/billTextClient.xhtml?bill_id=201920200AB730

282 See Chapter Five for a fuller discussion, in particular Article 52 Transparency obligations

283 This is distinct from the action taken against companies such as Clearview AI who are being restricted from such activity by breach of data and privacy related legislation

are still subject to resolution by ongoing litigation. There are however some interesting trends which are probably worth mentioning here.

The first is a recent decision by the US Supreme Court[284]. This may challenge the extent which the "fair use" doctrine in US Copyright Law can be relied upon by AI developers in relation to their AI generated works, on the basis that they "transform" the original work into something new.

In reviewing a 1984 painting entitled *Orange Prince* by Andy Warhol, the Supreme Court had to determine whether or not that work infringed the rights of photographer Lynn Goldsmith. The Court found that the work infringed those rights because Warhol's work was made for commercial gain and therefore could not rely on the fair use doctrine subsisting in US Copyright law.

Secondly, in the UK the Government recently responded to 2021 Intellectual Property Office consultation on Artificial Intelligence and Intellectual Property[285].

The initial outcomes of that consultation were that no changes to UK intellectual property law were proposed to either computer generated works or AI devised inventions. However a very wide text and data mining ("TDM") exemption was proposed, including for the purposes of training AI systems. Subsequently however, and in the face of vocal opposition from the creative industries, and given the extreme impact of generative AI, it now appears that the UK Government is rowing back from this very broad TDM exemption[286].

---

284 See *Andy Warhol Foundation for the Visual Arts v. Goldsmith SC 21-869, May 18th 2023*

285 Artificial Intelligence and Intellectual Property: copyright and patents: Government response to consultation, Updated 28 June 2022

286 See UK Parliamentary debate, 1st February 2023, comments from George Freeman, Minister of State for Science, Research and Innovation. https://hansard.parliament.uk/commons/2023-02-01/debates/7CD1D4F9-7805-4CF0-9698-

In summary we have learned that in the context of artificial intelligence, it is not sufficient to purely rely on the concepts of copyright and patents law – although these still remain fundamentally important, they do not provide one hundred percent coverage and protection for such systems.

Trade secret law also has a part to play in protecting investment in machine learning systems that have been taught, tuned and refined through a process of exposure to carefully curated data sets.

So far as the data sets themselves are concerned, you need to ensure (as owner or developer of a machine learning system) that you allow for *information residuals* to be retained by your system. As a licensor of third-party data sets to a machine learning system developer, you should consider how this fact is to be reflected commercially and legally in your licences.

E28ECEFB7177/ArtificialIntelligenceIntellectualPropertyRights

CHAPTER NINE

AUTOMATED BIAS AND DISCRIMINATION

One of the very powerful benefits of artificial intelligence when coupled with big data is the ability of such systems to make predictions or synthesise outputs based on the data which have been presented to them. There is an oft quoted popular fallacy which assumes infallibility and impartiality in such systems – in effect that they are immune from bias[287].

The partial truth of course is that whilst machines are generally impervious to human emotion when making decisions –as we shall see in this chapter, this does not necessarily equate to lack of subjectivity in such decisions.

AI systems are very dependent on the quality of the data that is fed into them – they need accurate and representative data sets in order to learn and refine their processing of their assigned application – whether that is on a supervised, unsupervised or reinforcement basis.

Being "*fed*" training data and ongoing operational data is critical to performance improvement and enhancement. This is sometimes referred to as the "*data diet vulnerability*".

A classic example of this (now thankfully rectified) was the original Google Translate algorithm. Rather than being "trained" in a conventional way to follow rules of linguistic grammar, Google Translate acquired its linguistic skills by parsing hundreds of thousands of texts, many of which were centuries old. As you can imagine, the prejudices and cultural stereotypes in those written works ended up being reflected

---

[287] See the discussion in Chapter Six on *automation bias*

in the translations produced by Google's system. This was particularly problematic in languages with non-specific gender references, as has been particularly well documented – so to take a particular example, if the original version of Google Translate was instructed to translate from English to Turkish and back to English again, the phrase "*HE is lazy*" was translated into "*SHE is lazy*", and the phrase "*SHE is smart*" would be translated to "*HE is smart*".

Clearly Google had to do something about this and they ended up creating a discrimination algorithm to potentially filter these culturally offensive outputs and provide alternatives where the immediate context was equivocal, ultimately a hugely complex task.[288]

The *data diet vulnerability* described above gives rise to another practical legal consideration in relation to the use of machine learning systems – that is the extent to which if such training and operational data sets do contain bias, or are skewed in a particular direction (to e.g. reinforce a specific outcome) they can give rise to automated decisions which are likely to prejudice or discriminate against individuals. In particular it also raises the question of how such bias should be managed at law.

It is an established fact that automating a process – or relegating it to technology can ironically (and somewhat perversely) act to *reduce* oversight in relation to bias thus perpetuating the fallacy of impartiality I describe above.

We are all conditioned to believe in the efficiency of computers. This is clearly a disturbing consideration (and one which should be constantly challenged) where such systems are using data that overtly refers to personally identifiable information. It is especially concerning when one considers that the vulnerability could be deliberately and malevolently exploited in order to make a system biased or discriminatory in addition

288 See a very revealing interview with Google's head of translation, Macduff Hughes: https://www.theverge.com/2019/1/30/18195909/google-translate-ai-machine-learning-bias-religion-macduff-hughes-interview

to the consequences of accidental "*skewing*"[289]. Remember also that the breadth of such impact should also be taken into account – consider our earlier discussion on the characteristics of data – discrimination or bias could result from data which indirectly refers to an individual or which is *inferred* or *derived* from other data.

In addition to the problem of training data sets "hard coding" bias into an artificially intelligent system, there is also the problem of the so-called "*filter bubble*" or "*echo chamber*" effect – which in reality is an extension of the algorithmic bias described above.

Filter bubble effects occur during operational use of AI systems as they learn and adapt outputs to user behaviour – these can act to reinforce or compound bias by serving up decisions and results which are within the data bubble and excluding those which are outside it – even when in some circumstances, the excluded results may be legitimate.

Typically filter bubbles are discussed in the context of intelligent web browsers that try to direct and focus search results based on previous internet browsing behaviour, but the analysis is equally valid in situations where an AI system has learned (through application of data sets) to select or make choices in a distinct manner.

As we have previously discussed, Microsoft's Tay, a bulletin board chatbot launched in 2016, but rapidly and subsequently withdrawn, was a classic example of this. Tay quickly adopted the characteristics of the boards it was posting on and developed overt racist and xenophobic tendencies. It was merely reflecting the unpleasant demographic of the boards it was posting on[290].

Another example which particularly illustrates these problems is in

[289] This is a very real concern of EU Parliamentarians that have considerably strengthened these provisions in the latest draft of the EU Artificial Intelligence Act – see Chapter Five

[290] See: https://www.techrepublic.com/article/why-microsofts-tay-ai-bot-went-wrong/

relation to automated recruitment. The recruitment industry has embraced automation wholeheartedly – especially in relation to those jobs which are perceived as commoditised or where the industry must achieve large scale volume recruitment for clients in short timescales. Sectors where there is high demand for interim employment also find such automated approaches attractive. The net result has been a boom in the development of systems that can automate selection and rejection of CVs, right the way through to chatbots or robotic interviewers that can lead discussions and filter candidates.

Whilst no one doubts the efficiency of such systems when properly implemented, there are concerns that exclusive dependence on them could, aside from the potential for discrimination and bias described above, lead to recruitment which is based purely on documented skills (via CVs) ignoring softer metrics such as an individual's personality, fit and emotional temperament. A classic example of this was an algorithmic system employed by Amazon to automate recruitment in 2015 (but subsequently quietly withdrawn). It was discovered that the system had taught itself to prefer male candidates over female candidates, allegedly because the relevant models were trained to vet applications over a historic ten-year period – during which time most had been men, reflecting the overwhelmingly traditional male dominance of the technology industry[291]. This is but one example however – there are many instances in modern society where we are increasingly ceding complex decisions to machine learning systems which relate to such diverse matters as the finance we can obtain to the news we read.

The GDPR

So far as the law itself is concerned, the General Data Protection Regulation provides a framework in relation to machine-based decisions. The greatest potential impact for individuals is of course in relation to those decisions that have "*legal affects that significantly affect data*

291 See https://www.reuters.com/article/us-amazon-com-jobs-automation-insight-idUSKCN1MK08G

subjects"[292] – and it is in this context and in the context of profiling[293] which the GDPR attempts to address – see the commentary in Chapter Six above.

Clearly automated bias and discrimination was one of the problems that the GDPR was implemented to address. We have already discussed the key principles that apply in these circumstances but it is worth covering generally what the GDPR provides for both in terms of punitive sanctions against controllers and processors that breach the provisions of the regulation and individual remedies for EU citizens who have been unfairly discriminated against – or made the subject of bias.

The GDPR significantly increases the levels of administrative fines that can be levied on data controllers and expands this punitive regime to data processors for the first time. Clearly the amounts of such fines will depend upon the individual circumstances of the particular case and a number of other factors, such as the seriousness of the breach and the extent to which the breach has been repeated[294] but it is evident that European legislators intended the obligations relating to profiling and automated decision making[295] to be subject to an increased level of sanction – up to the higher of 20m or 4% of the total worldwide annual turnover of an undertaking[296].

We have already seen in Chapter Six that data controllers which carry out profiling or automated decision making (as defined by Article 22 of the GDPR) can only do so on the basis of the explicit consent of the data subject[297] and that such consent can be withdrawn at any time. Data

---

[292] Article 22 – GDPR

[293] Article 4(4) GDPR

[294] See Article 83(2)(a)-(k) GDPR for a complete list of qualifying factors

[295] Article 22 GDPR

[296] Article 83(5)(b) GDPR

[297] Article 22(2)(a)-(b) provide for additional carve outs related to the performance of contract obligations and specific authorisations of a Member State, see earlier

subjects have additional rights to rectification[298] – including the right to obtain from a data controller without undue delay, the rectification of inaccurate personal data relating to them (in addition to the right to have incomplete or partial data on them completed), as well as a right to erasure (the so called "*right to be forgotten*")[299]. This is all in addition to a right to direct compensation for data subjects which is enshrined in Article 82 of the Regulation.

It is evident there are a comprehensive suite of remedies and sanctions that are available to counter potential bias and discrimination in relation to processing under the GDPR. However there remains a major concern about identifying whether and how such bias has taken place, which is often very hard to determine, particularly when machine learning technology is involved. Bias and discrimination are key areas which demand further research from machine learning scientists to develop solutions that can audit – or provide a full explanation for – their decisions.

As we learned in Chapters One and Two the industry is not yet in a position to find convincing technological solutions to provide this explanatory functionality, especially where "*black box*" AI systems are used, although there are clear industry research initiatives to enable it.

The EU Artificial Intelligence Act

The draft EU Artificial Intelligence Act recognises bias as a major compliance requirement for AI and as such this is reflected both as a new general underlying principle introduced in the latest EU Parliament Text version[300] and as a key obligation for "high risk" AI systems deployed within the EU – albeit qualified in the latest version of the draft to

Chapter Six

[298] Article 16 GDPR

[299] Article 17 GDPR

[300] See Article 4 a of the EU Artificial Intelligence Act and discussion in Chapter Five

techniques that are within the current "*state of the art*"[301].

The Equality Act 2010

The other potential legal consequences that should be considered in relation to the use of artificially intelligent systems in the UK revolve principally around the Equality Act 2010.

The Equality Act is a consolidating measure in the UK which brings together the former principles set out in predecessor legislation: the Equal Pay Act 1970, the Sex Discrimination Act 1975, the Race Relations Act 1976 and the Disability Discrimination Act 1995, as well as updating the law to provide for age discrimination.

Undoubtedly the Equality Act has a part to play in determining whether or not discrimination has taken place in the workplace and in wider society – its provisions are particularly relevant to the issue of automated bias that are the subject of this chapter. There is a substantial concern however that the law as drafted however does not *explicitly* allow for a right to understand the basis for decisions made by machine learning systems.[302] The Equality Act is frustratingly unclear when it discusses burden of proof in relation to prohibited conduct, particularly when considering the nature and circumstances of algorithmic selection and decision making by artificially intelligent systems which (as we have already discussed in the context of Chapter Four above) do not directly translate human actions into machine outputs. Section 136 of the Act for example provides that "*If there are facts from which the court would decide, in the absence of any other explanation, that person (A) contravened the provision concerned, the court must hold that the contravention occurred.*"[303].

---

301 See in particular discussion on Article 12 1 of the EU Artificial Intelligence Act in Chapter Five

302 See for example the report of the Future of Work Commission, December 2017 (commissioned by the Labour Party)

303 s136 (2)

Generally, Section 136 dictates an absolutist and relatively unsubtle approach – it does not really address concerns about AI transparency – the use of automated machine learning tools to make opaque selection decisions which could potentially be discriminatory and where direct human intervention in such decisions may be limited.

Until this position is clarified, we are in the awkward position of relying on the general rights we have described above under the GDPR and extrapolating the Equality Act's current drafting into our immediate context to see how it might apply. As before, our discussion is based on an analysis of the use of machine learning technologies in this context and I do not propose to provide a comprehensive summary of the Act.

What we are concerned about here is the potential for an AI system that is responsible for decision making, choices and selection to directly or indirectly discriminate against an individual's "*protected characteristics*", as these are defined through the introduction of bias in training or operational data. We have already established the potential for such machine learning systems to make decisions which due to the complexity of their processing capabilities can be incredibly difficult to rationalise on a human explicable basis and also that the learned behaviours they exhibit can "*skew*" decisions in a particular direction (the so-called *filter bubble* effect we discussed earlier).

The Equality Act itself creates a number of obligations which can lead to civil and potential criminal consequences. Criminal causation and artificial intelligence is a topic we consider specifically in Chapter Ten – which should be reviewed if you are interested in a more in-depth analysis of machine commissioned offences. So far as this chapter is concerned, we'll consider the prohibited acts contemplated by the Act and the provisions of Schedule 25[304], which provide some indirect pointers as to what types of machine processing are specifically excluded from its provisions.

---

[304] Information Society Service Providers

The Equality Act makes the following "*protected characteristics*" – age[305], disability[306], gender reassignment[307], marriage and civil partnership[308], race[309], religion or belief[310], sex[311] and sexual orientation[312]. It then specifies several types of prohibited conduct in relation to those protected characteristics, which fall within Direct Discrimination[313] – being treated less favourably directly or overtly on the basis of possessing one of these protected characteristics (for example being denied a promotion on the basis of homosexuality) and Indirect Discrimination[314] – often unintended, where a provision, criterion or practice is applied equally to a group but which will ostensibly have the indirect effect of putting those who have the protected characteristic at a disadvantage.

Indirect discrimination is probably the most concerning from the perspective of machine learning given our description above, in that it is the situation which is most likely to occur when a generalised algorithmic approach is applied to a class of people. This is conduct which appears neutral but when applied to someone with a protected characteristic puts them at a disadvantage[315]. It is also worth mentioning that there are additional prohibited acts relating to Harassment[316] (unwanted conduct

305 s5

306 s6

307 s7

308 s8

309 s9

310 s10

311 s11

312 s12

313 s13

314 s19

315 Note our earlier discussion in Chapter Five on the expanded classes of Prohibited AI introduced by the Artificial Intelligence Act (EU Parliament Text). In particular a new class of prohibited categorisation on the basis of biometric characteristics, see Article 5 1 b a (Amendment 217) of the EU Parliament Text.

316 s26

by someone against another (or overtly sexual conduct) which degrades the victim or creates a humiliating or offensive situation) and perhaps less relevant to this discussion, Victimisation[317] (essentially detrimental treatment triggered by 'whistleblowing').

The Act applies to those parties carrying out the prohibited conduct (generally in an employment context, this will be an employer) but in addition also applies to "*service providers*". Service Providers are defined as those " *...concerned with the provision of a service to the public or a section of the public (for payment or not)*"[318].

It is important to note that a service provider for the purposes of the Act may not necessarily correspond with an AI provider in the narrow sense that we are discussing for the purposes of this chapter, but equally speaking *might.*

Service providers under the Equality Act provide any service. So for example when in 2015 a female paediatrician was allegedly unable to access the female changing rooms at her gym (because the automated swipe card system had incorrectly correlated the title "Dr" to exclusively male members), the Gym provider (the service provider in this context) could have been liable for directly discriminating against her on the basis of her sex[319].

The provider of an AI system could conceivably be a service provider for the purposes of the Equality Act if offering a service directly to the public. In a non-public context (for example, where an employer has licensed the use of a machine learning system as a tool for use within its own business), it seems likely that employers will also be fixed with liability for the consequences of their machine learning systems in addition to any potential liability which the AI provider might also accrue. Section

317 s27

318 s29

319 https://www.dailymail.co.uk/news/article-3000705/Female-paediatrician-locked-gym-changing-room-computer-assumed-Doctor-title-MAN.html

109(2) of the Equality Act provides that "*Anything done by an agent for a principal, with the authority of the principal, must be treated as **also** being done by the principal*" (emphasis added).

For the purposes of the Act, there is an important liability distinction as between service providers and employers in that whilst employers have a defence to a claim for discrimination on the basis that they take all reasonable steps to prevent it from arising[320], service providers are automatically fixed with the consequences of using technology. In practical terms this means of course that such service providers should consider very carefully the use of such technology in the provision of their service. As we have already seen, given the very complex nature of artificially intelligent systems it would be prudent in such circumstances for guarantees to be obtained from the machine learning provider that there are no instances of inbuilt bias or prejudice in their system and if and to the extent such does occur, contractual remedies, such as indemnities and other financial recompense, should be available.

Service providers may avoid liability under the Equality Act if they fall within the definition of "*Information Society Service Providers*" under Schedule 25, but in practical terms it seems clear that any utility of this provision to artificial intelligence providers is vanishingly slight.

Information Society Services are defined by the UK E-Commerce regulations[321] as "*any service normally provided for remuneration at a distance, by means of electronic equipment for the processing (including digital compression) and storage of data, at the individual request of a recipient of the service.*" Obviously the provisions of the Equality Act and the E-Commerce regulations were drafted before the advent of meaningful developments in artificial intelligence and machine learning. Some machine learning solutions will not fall within this definition, but

---

[320] s109(4)

[321] Electronic Commerce (EC Directive) Regulations 2002 implementing the EU Electronic Commerce Directive 2002, repeated in Schedule 25 paragraph 7 (1) (2) (b)

it is conceivable that a subscription-based machine learning service might. At the time Schedule 25 was intended to ensure that most online businesses within the EU were excluded from the operation of the Equality Act to the extent they were acting as a "*mere conduit*"[322] – providing access to a communications network or transmission within a communication network of information; a "*cache*"[323] – providing a temporary storage facility purely to facilitate the onwards transmission of information or a "*host*"[324] – storing information provided by a recipient of the service.

Crucially for the purposes of our analysis, Schedule 25 exemptions are removed in the case of conduits *"if the information is stored for longer than is reasonably necessary for the transmission"*[325] and in the case of caching if the service provider "*does not modify the information*"[326], both conditions of which it seems likely would be transgressed by the provider of a typical AI system.

So what are the remedies that are available to individuals that have been discriminated against? UK Tribunals and courts have various powers available to them, the most significant of which is that they can award compensation for both financial losses and what are termed "injury to feelings" awards. Such bodies can also make declarations and recommendations.

Compensation can technically be awarded against both a company and an individual perpetrator, although in the case of automated/AI decisions, this is obviously likely to be less relevant. *Injury to feelings* damages are awarded on what is known as the Vento scale[327]. This

---

322 Paragraph 3, Schedule 25 EA 2010

323 Paragraph 4, Schedule 25 EA 2010

324 Paragraph 5, Schedule 25 EA 2010

325 Paragraph 3 (4), Schedule 25

326 Paragraph 4 (3) (a), Schedule 25

327 Named after *Vento v. Chief Constable of West Yorkshire Police* [2002] EWCA Civ

generally prescribes three "bands" – the lower band, which applies to less serious cases where the act of discrimination is a one off or isolated occurrence; the middle band which applies to serious cases that do not fall within the higher band; and the higher band which applies in the most serious cases, for example where there has been a lengthy campaign of discrimination and/or harassment. Typically in most service provision cases, the tendency has been to award such damages in in the lower band, as such cases of discrimination tend to be one off, isolated incidents.

"Fake News" and other data biases

The foregoing sections of this chapter cover laws on discrimination generally – assessing liability for the users of AI systems that make decisions which have *real* and significant consequences for *real* people. One should not however underestimate the potential for machine learning to continue to permeate within and influence other aspects of our lives less directly and in doing so the corresponding potential for it to spread "*data bias*" as well.

One particular example springs to mind – new digital media is a specific case in point where the assembly of "custom" news items can lead to the filter bubble effect we described above. In more extreme cases there is the potential for ill-intentioned state actors to influence media content by so called "fake news" – indeed there continues to be much publicity to this effect in relation to the US presidential election of 2020.

Artificially intelligent machines are taking increasing responsibility for actually writing and assembling "news" or social media items automatically and are capable of expertly manipulating photo-realistic images with no noticeable artefacts. As we saw in Chapter Eight, this has been taken to extreme lengths recently through the creation of machine learning neural network software that can be trained to substitute one face for another in a segment of video – so called "*deep fakes*", some of

1871 which established the principles

which are extremely convincing and latterly disturbing.

The EU Artificial Intelligence Act does explicitly recognise this trend as a particular concern, and directly introduces provisions to regulate deep fakes[328]. Whether this legislation will have any substantive impact in this context (particularly given the bad faith of many actors creating such content) remains to be seen.

328 See Article 52 of the EU AIA (EU Parliament Text), and discussion in Chapter Five

CHAPTER TEN

AI CRIME: COMMISSION AND JUDGMENT

We look at two aspects of criminal liability in this Chapter. The first is to examine the realistic potential for artificially intelligent systems to be liable under criminal law for the commission of an offence. The second, and I suspect rather less theoretical question, is to examine the extent to which artificial intelligence systems are influencing sentencing and bail decisions made in relation to those within the criminal justice system.

In Chapter Four we looked at the legal theory of causation in a civil context – principally through the filters of tort, contract and product liability. Criminal causation is inevitably and inexorably linked to this discussion. Necessarily our debate will touch on robots in addition to artificial intelligence. As we discovered in Chapter One, modern day robots may share some characteristics with disembodied machine learning systems if they have enabled machine learning software elements – the additional factor of course is that they interact *physically* with the real world which gives them the potential to undertake *physical* acts which could lead to criminal consequences in the real world.

Pure machine learning systems in contrast are constrained by digital barriers in relation to the criminal consequences they could potentially create, although given current cybercrime levels this does not make an analysis of such systems in this context any less relevant, particularly so as those digital barriers become more permeable and connectivity between systems and smart-functionality becomes more and more ubiquitous.

Crimes at their most basic interpretation are of course acts which are deemed – either through the application of common law or by statute –

as abhorrent or contrary to the normal functioning of society, the commission of which brings about a punitive consequence. Taking aside strict liability offences, there are three basic prerequisites for criminal liability to be established in human actors – the ***Actus Reus*** – or criminal act; the ***Mens Rea*** – or criminal intent (the so-called guilty mind), and ***concurrence*** or ***coincidence*** – the coincidence of both of the former. Liability cannot be established generally unless the actor has a guilty mind and in tandem perpetrates the criminal deed.

The Actus Reas element as we know can be expressed by acts or omissions and the Mens Rea element has various levels ranging from knowledge and specific intent all the way to criminal negligence or "recklessness".

So far as machine-based liability itself is concerned, there are essentially three models which have been debated by commentators and bear analysis – the first does not impute any special characteristics to the AI system.

Instrumental extension

The "*instrumental extension*" model treats AI as a tool or instrumental extension of the perpetrator, which is where the real criminal liability is focussed. This model works well, as in civil causation, where the actions of the machine are directly attributable to the actions of its user. Conventional computers, and indeed most inanimate objects, are particularly suited to this linear causality. Take for example the scenario of an entirely "dumb" factory robot, which through the direct controlled actions of its user, manages to kill a factory worker. The robot here has direct equivalence with a knife or a gun. Provided the user has the requisite *mens rea*, it seems likely that the elements of murder will be established.

The requirement of concurrence has also evolved in English jurisprudence to cover not just temporal concurrence but also motivational concurrence – provided that the guilty actor has the motivation to carry out the crime, it is not necessary for the *actus reus* to coincide in time. Many crimes are in fact the product of a sequence of connected events leading to the commission of an offence[329]. Taking our earlier example of a "dumb" robot, it seems likely therefore that even if our user had programmed the robot *earlier* to behave in a particular way likely to cause the death of the factory worker (in the full knowledge that the factory worker would be present at that time) he would not escape criminal liability.

Machine Learning systems however are one step removed from this. As we have seen, they are not directly programmed but rather trained, over a period of time, in relation to a particular task. As we discussed in Chapter One, their learning can be influenced by appropriate data sets but their behaviours (or outputs) are not directed by prescriptive programmed instructions. By their very nature, many such systems are inherently opaque. There are of course likely to be examples of criminality where this disconnection will be problematic from an evidential point of view – especially if for example, the object of the criminal actors is to use machine learning tools to obfuscate or hide their criminal activities and more specifically (and problematically) their criminal *intent* – e.g. in a complex money laundering case (in this regard it is important to remember the distinction between burdens of proof in criminal cases and civil ones – whereas a civil case need be proved only on a *balance of probabilities*, the evidential burden in criminal cases is much higher – *beyond reasonable doubt*).

In other cases however, this disconnect is likely to be relatively meaningless given the context and circumstances – take the 2015 case (publicised somewhat melodramatically in the media as "*Robot gets arrested*") of a Swiss art collective that used an intelligent "bot" armed with $100 worth of bitcoin to purchase Ecstasy tablets, a Hungarian Passport and various spying devices as part of an art installation on the power of the so called "Dark Web". The system (called "*Random Dark*

329 See for example *R v. Le Brun [1991] CA*; *R v. Jakeman (1982) CA*; *Fagan v. Metropolitan Police Commissioner [1968] QBD*

Net Shopper") purchased the items and had them delivered to the art gallery – a relatively easy way to track down the perpetrators.[330]

Natural and probable consequences

The next model which has been proposed in the context of machine liability is what is termed the "*natural probable consequences*" model. I should say at the outset that this is a highly problematic doctrine in its own right and has been largely discredited in many US states, as well as comparable jurisdictions, such as the UK which expressly prohibited its application by s8 of the Criminal Justice Act 1967[331].

Under this doctrine, the AI system takes action which is a "*natural and probable*" consequence of its training. So going back to our earlier example of the robot killing a factory worker, (assuming our machine now has artificial intelligence capabilities), in this doctrine, the creator of the artificially intelligent system does not need to have a specific intent (or *mens rea*) to kill the factory worker, but rather a state of criminal negligence – that is to say reckless disregard as to whether the training of the machine learning system could lead to the death of the factory worker – if a reasonable person in the place of the creator could have forseen the offence as a *natural probable consequence* of the way in which the process was conducted. The doctrine evolved as a way to embrace accomplice liability (i.e. where there been offence committed by an accomplice which is not part of a conspiracy, but which would otherwise be a "natural probable consequence" of a criminal scheme) and essentially side steps the subjective requirement for juries to assess whether or not the guilty party possessed the necessary mens rea. Ironically, given the difficulties we have discussed above in relation to the opaque way in which machine learning systems operate, this doctrine (although effectively discredited)

---

330 See Guardian dated 22 April 2015 "*Swiss Police release robot that bought ecstasy online*"

331 s8 of the 1967 Act reversed the position reached in *DPP v. Smith (1961) AC 290* which originally proposed a "natural and probable consequences" test as a means to attempt to objectively translate criminal recklessness into intent

might in fact provide a more convenient route for the judicial system to establish appropriate criminal liability in cases where artificially intelligent systems have been used in the commission of an offence.

Direct machine liability

Finally, there is the theoretical possibility of a criminal liability model which assumes some level of responsibility *per se* on the part of the machine for its actions. I refer to theoretical because, as we have learned, liability and accountability both require some element of understanding and self-awareness on the part of the artificially intelligent system for the consequences of its actions.

To a certain degree this plays back to our debate on individuation in the context of civil causation in Chapter Four. Despite the views of many populist commentators, we are not currently at a technological state of the art where this is relevant.

How then should the criminal justice system respond to increasingly complex crimes in which increasingly complex machines play significant parts? The response must logically be dictated in a similar manner to the conclusions I reach in Chapter Four – if the natural and probable consequence doctrine cannot be reinvigorated in criminal situations where machine intelligence is deployed, potentially making the issue of determining whether the alleged defendants to a crime have the requisite *mens rea,* then the response of the legislators has to be to consider an increase in the scope of strict liability offences.

Strict liability

Generally strict liability offences are those under which intention does not have to be proven in relation to an aspect of the *actus reus*, although some element of intent may be required in relation to the other aspects of the offence in question – such as recklessness. Strict liability offences are as a rule created by Statute – however typically, Parliament does not make it expressly clear in most instances whether an offence should be one of strict liability. Indeed this may be an unintended consequence of some Acts which are poorly drafted or vague in their approach.

The courts apply several principles to override the general presumption of *mens rea* to establish strict liability[332]. For the purposes of our current analysis, it makes sense to focus on these principles which are likely to come into sharp focus in circumstances where use of intelligent machines cause injury or loss, and that is where a statutory offence is dealing with an issue of social concern.

The leading case of *Gammon (Hong Kong) v. AG*[333] provides that where a statute is legislating on an issue of social concern, and the creation of strict liability will promote the purpose of the statute by encouraging individuals to take extra measures against committing the offence, the general presumption in favour of mens rea can be rebutted.

Typically the courts will not make this leap where the offence is a "real" crime with moral consequences as opposed to an offence which is regulatory in nature[334] (usually one where no moral issues are involved) or one which carries serious penalties – generally they are more willing to do so in cases where the penalties for breach are relatively small – but this is not a rule which is applied prescriptively.

The Gammon case concerned a failure on the part of the defendants to follow building plans accurately (due to the imposition of changes) which caused a major building collapse in Hong Kong. Under the relevant building and construction regulations there was a maximum penalty for breach of up to three years in prison or a fine of $250,000. The Privy Council upheld the view that the offence was one of strict liability and it did not matter whether the defendants were aware that their changes may have led to the collapse.

---

332 In *B (a minor) v. DPP (2000)*

333 [1985] AC 1

334 See *Sweet v. Parsley [1970] AC 132*

As the use of artificially intelligent systems becomes more pervasive in society, so inevitably the tendency of the clever and ill-intentioned to avoid criminal sanctions will increase commensurately and of course in many clever, convoluted and devious ways that cannot be predicted. The extension of strict liability could provide society with an organic and flexible response to these changing circumstances which do not necessitate a wholesale change to the way in which we judge criminal accountability.

The criminal justice system – bail and sentencing decisions

The second part of this chapter takes a look at the increasing use of machine learning systems in the criminal justice system – specifically in relation to the sentencing of crimes. The increased uptake of such systems raises the spectres of bias, discrimination and accountability (and the increased potential for claims which are based on the misuse of such systems) which we have discussed in previous chapters but which it is important to discuss in the context of crime.

In the criminal justice system, artificial intelligence is now being used in the United States and the United Kingdom to make sentencing, bail and parole decisions for prisoners. Interestingly, and as noted in Chapter Five earlier, this practice, to the extent AI is used to calculate risks of recidivism, is likely to fall within a Prohibited AI use case under the proposed Artificial Intelligence Act and therefore will be unlawful throughout the European Union[335].

The US criminal case of *State v. Loomis*[336], provides a somewhat worrying example of the rise of such technology (and the court's attitude to its use). Eric Loomis was charged in early 2015 with five criminal counts in a drive by shooting in Wisconsin. In the event, the defendant pleaded guilty to two lesser of the five charges. In preparation for his sentencing

335 See EU Parliament Text version of the AIA, Article 5 1 d a (amendment 224)

336 881 N.W. 2d 749 (Wis. 2016)

hearing, the Wisconsin Department of Corrections produced a pre-sentencing investigation report (a so called "PSI"), that included an AI assessment of his potential to commit further crime.

The system used in Loomis' assessment was COMPAS, developed by Equivant. COMPAS is a decision tree-based classification solution and uses interviews with offenders as well as information from their criminal records history to determine the risk of recidivism. As such it is employed primarily in the US criminal justice system to assess eligibility for parole, bail and also to determine sentencing levels.

Ironically, given the nature of the algorithmic solution, which is more white box than black box (see our discussions in Chapters One and Two), both Loomis and the Court were prevented from obtaining details as to how the system had classified him for sentencing on the basis that the methodology the system used was proprietary in nature – specifically a trade secret.

The Wisconsin Supreme Court found that the defendant's due process had not been violated by use of an algorithmic sentencing system, even though it was not made clear to the defendant or the court *how* it had reached the conclusions it had in his particular case. Instead, the court ruled that any future use of such automated assessments needed to be subject to notification of certain "health warnings". These health warnings should be directed to the court reviewing the system's decisions in any particular situation in order to prevent blind acceptance of its findings and to introduce a degree of judicial scepticism. Whilst this approach clearly acknowledges the risk of relying on algorithmic risk assessment, it provided cold comfort for the defendant in the Loomis case. It is particularly interesting to note that this case is unlikely to have been decided in an equivalent manner in the EU – even if perhaps the outcome of the case might have been the same.

Article 22 of the GDPR on Automated Decision making and profiling prevents (as we have seen previously in Chapter Six) cursory human involvement in such decision making and would require active and participative involvement in the part of the judges involved when making a sentencing decision.

CHAPTER ELEVEN

MARKET DISTORTING EFFECTS: AI AND COMPETITION LAW

Competition and trade sit at the heart of western democratic societies. The fundamental principles enshrined in the European Union's 1958 Treaty of Rome – now the "*TFEU*" or "*Treaty on the functioning of the EU*" have as their bases the general aspiration that within the European Union, trade should be unfettered and that goods and services be allowed to develop market equilibrium free of behaviours such as organised *cartels* (companies coming together in a concerted fashion to maintain or fix prices or share markets or customers or otherwise distort market forces) or the *abuse of a dominant market position* (using a monopoly position to exploit customers or to entrench that monopoly).

Again, I do not propose within this chapter to provide a comprehensive guide to competition law (there are other more detailed texts which achieve this aim), but rather to contextualise our debate on machine learning within the framework of competition law rules and provide you the reader with an appreciation of the issues which might apply when using AI tools in this setting.

Competition law is a public interest driven exception to the principle of freedom of contract. Effective competition typically drives lower prices, better quality and choice and more innovation, so it is in the public – (ie. the consumer's) interest that companies do not co-operate or collude in ways which impede the free play of those market forces of competition.

Powerful machine learning tools can be deployed to increase the individual economic efficiency of undertakings. Reducing your cost base is a pro-competitive move which (absent dominance), competition law will not interfere with. But if such tools are used in a co-ordinated way, or if the agreement between the business and the AI supplier contains restrictions on competition (such as, for example, exclusivity provisions or "*most favoured customer*" clauses, then there may be regulatory tension in relation to the permissible use of such tools in an economic context.

Article 101(1) TFEU[337] provides that "*The following shall be prohibited as incompatible with the internal market: all agreements between undertakings, decisions by associations of undertakings and concerted practices which may affect trade between Member States and which have as their object or effect the prevention, restriction or distortion of competition...and in particular those which: (a) directly or indirectly fix purchase or selling prices...; (b) limit or control production, markets, technical development, or investment; (c) share markets or sources of supply;* [and/or] *(d) apply dissimilar conditions to equivalent transactions with other trading parties, thereby placing them at a competitive disadvantage; (e)...*". Article 101(3) provides for the derogation to this overarching principle (where the agreement, decision or concerted practice of undertakings may be allowed) if it "*contributes to improving the production or distribution of goods or to promoting technical or economic progress, while allowing consumers a fair share of the resulting benefit*" and does not either impose unnecessary restrictions (ie. those indispensable to the objectives expressed in Article 101(3))[338] or provide such undertakings with the possibility of "*eliminating competition*" for a substantial part of the products in question[339]. Article 102 TFEU then goes on to explain the European Union position on abuses of a dominant market position: "*Any abuse by one or more undertakings of a dominant position within the internal market ... shall be prohibited as incompatible with the internal market in so far as it may affect trade between Member States. Such abuse may, in*

337 Post-Brexit, much of the EU competition law regime has effectively been 'mirrored' in English law, see Chapters I and II of the Competition Act 1998 as amended by the Competition (Amendment etc.) (EU Exit) Regulations 2019, SI 2019 No. 93

338 See Article 101(3)(a) TFEU

339 See Article 101(3)(B) TFEU

particular, consist in: (a) directly or indirectly imposing unfair purchase or selling prices or other unfair trading conditions; (b) limiting production, markets or technical development to the prejudice of consumers; [and/or] *(c) applying dissimilar conditions to equivalent transactions with other trading parties, thereby placing them at a competitive disadvantage; (d) ....*". There are derogations from these overarching principles (such as for example in relation to agricultural trade between the EU Member States – protecting the Common Agricultural Policy; in relation to the Defence industry; and finally intellectual property licensing), but I do not propose to dwell on these here. Additionally, the United States has similar, but not precisely equivalent provisions in its anti-trust legislation, predominantly enshrined in the Sherman Act[340].

The essential question to understand for the purposes of this text is to understand how the use of machine learning tools can undermine these central principles and if so, in what manner. The essence of our debate in this context has similarities with, and draws from, our previous discussions in relation to bias and discrimination (Chapter Nine) and big data (Chapter Six). Put simply, machine learning systems have the ability to analyse and correlate hugely complex pools of data and review dimensionalities in such data which are far beyond what could be achieved by humans in any realistic timeline.

As we move completely into digital data processing and away from an essentially analog documentary existence, vast amounts of data have become available to information processing systems. It is not just the ability to spot patterns at a superhuman level which is interesting from a competition law perspective, but also the ability of such systems to make autonomous decisions and react on the basis of such data almost instantaneously.

[340] See sections 1 and 2 of the Sherman Act 1890

Pro-competitive vs. anti-competitive effects

The impact of machine learning on anti-trust and competition principles creates a uniquely polarised duality, and one which is highly market specific. One of the best ways to illustrate this and to show how such technologies can act potentially both as a competition enabler and blocker is to look at an industry specific contextual example.

As we saw in Chapter Six, in the context of our discussion on big data, the insurance industry has been one of the trailblazers for use of machine learning technology. Artificial intelligence is rapidly transforming the way in which insurance is priced, quoted for and underwritten. Increasing sophistication is allowing new insurance intermediary start-ups to model synthetic claims data to enable much more accurate pricing of risk. As these intermediaries gather more and more actual claims data (and more insurers participate in these intermediary platforms), their machine learning solutions become ever more accurate. The competitive impact of such tools depends upon who is deploying them: access to smaller underwriters may enable them to compete more efficiently in the market – effectively levelling the playing field, whilst price competition between the larger players may reduce if multiple parties use the same algorithmic pricing output.

In many situations the availability of online tools, such as price aggregation services and online commerce platforms drive healthy competition by forcing the market to respond in a number of ways: by for example, increasing pricing transparency and creating new routes to market for smaller businesses, reducing barriers to entry in a marketplace. To take a particular example if (ignoring for the moment the numerous regulatory hurdles involved) you have a mobile phone and a car, you can now compete with a taxi driver through driving apps such as Uber.

Product and service aggregation sites can act to facilitate competition by providing consumers with more easily accessible choice (indeed in some markets we now have aggregators that sit over multiple other aggregators to further enhance choice and price, such as SkyScanner[341], which essentially "sweeps" price aggregation data for airline tickets and flights from other aggregators). Finally artificial intelligence is fuelling an increasingly dynamic environment where pricing for goods and services can be adjusted in accordance with a number of complex external supply and demand factors – both actual and now predicted, on a near instantaneous basis to ensure that the most competitive pricing is offered in a way that would be inconceivable in a predominantly physical ("*bricks and mortar*") environment.

This essentially pro-competitive and beneficial view of digital competitive trends is however qualified by the reality of many competitive marketplaces which are dominated by a single monopolistic, or a few large oligopolistic, players. Businesses such as Google have seen significant fines for behaviour which the European Commission judges to be anti-competitive and damaging to its customers and/or the structure of competition.

Companies are increasingly realising that algorithms and big data are the fuel that drives their businesses and the key which will enable them to unlock more business and outperform their competitors. In many areas of modern business therefore it is as much about a race to obtain and secure large amounts of data in relation to the consumers of your products and services as it is about identifying pricing trends in those items.

Artificially intelligent systems put data acquisition and data manipulation on another, higher, much more sophisticated plane – not only can they analyse data as I have already described, but now they can also apply analytics to synthesise or predict data (as we saw in the context of Chapter Six above) which will determine pricing, availability, demand trends and other likely contextual information about the goods and services in question. Indeed, algorithmic systems are now being used to "*micro*

---

341 See www.skyscanner.net

target" consumers so that it is possible that you will be offered different pricing (when compared to another consumer) for the same service or product based on your perceived demand for it or some other characteristic, such as where you live, or be offered complementary products to those you have actually purchased.

Consider as well that much of this sophistication is offered within "*walled-garden*" ecosystems that have been developed by companies such as Amazon and eBay which have become so powerful that they cannot be ignored by other retailers (who in consequence, have to join them) and rather than enhanced competition, what might be happening is a recipe for consumers to have their choices limited either because they become bound to a single dominant marketplace or in the alternative are limited to using a few dominant players in an oligopoly.

In each case listed above there is in fact limited or no effective price competition – either because in the former, the *walled garden* can ultimately determine its own price equilibrium, which could potentially signal price monopolisation or in the latter where our oligopolistic players reach price stabilisation (or *harmonised* prices), not through any overt collusive activity, but simply because the algorithmic systems used by them have reached the same conclusion – in competition terms, through a process of *unconscious parallelism*.

These are of course polarised examples of the potential market effects of AI on economic activity – the world is a messy place and in reality the effect of artificial intelligence systems on trade and competition will need to be assessed on the facts of the individual case. We have not yet reached a unity in the deployment of artificial intelligence systems or indeed in terms of utilised data sets – as we have seen there are a variety of technological solutions being continuously developed and enhanced, and the reality is that different businesses gain different advantages from the use of these new tools. Such price and cost asymmetries will aid in the maintenance of a healthily competitive market. On the other hand, we cannot ignore the fact that in many markets the cost of entry is increasingly being driven by big data acquisition which, of itself, could prove a much higher barrier.

One of the biggest issues for anti-trust regulators in this context will of course be to spot and identify potentially insidious *automated* anti-competitive behaviours as we increasingly move into a digitalised environment.

Since the publication of the last edition of this book, it would not be an exaggeration to state that there has been an exponential increase in the use of machine learning in the trade and retail sectors. This has been accompanied by corresponding degrees of enhanced sophistication in the application of questionable manipulative techniques, many of which are complex and difficult from a regulatory perspective to analyse and track. It is worth spending some time analysing a selection of these techniques and behaviours and then examining what the appropriate regulatory responses have been to date.

Dark Patterns

This term, specifically referenced in a 2019 paper[342] but initially coined by UX designer Harry Brignull in 2010, refer to the interface designs created by online services that are created to steer or deceive users psychologically into making unintended and potentially harmful decisions, or rather more bluntly "*tricks used in websites and apps that make you buy or sign up for things that you didn't mean to*"[343].

Dark patterns exploit human behaviours in incredibly subtle ways. They are therefore particularly difficult in isolation to pinpoint as potentially anti-competitive behaviours but combined can have significant impact on online retail performance. There are countless examples of dark patterns, such as burying critical functions which may harm the on-line

342 *Dark Patterns at scale: Findings from a crawl of 11K shopping websites* Proc. ACM Hum.-Comput. Interact., Vol. 3, No. CSCW, Article 81

343 Brignull – see www.darkpatterns.org

service – Brignull's so called "*Roach Motel*" technique[344], to use of faked blotches, hairs or marks on banners to induce users of touchscreen enabled devices to touch and hence click on them. Algorithmic interference can enhance these techniques, for example by amplifying scarcity messages on hotel websites to encourage impulse booking, or providing misleading price comparisons between hotels, such as those posted on sites such as Trivago, which itself has been the subject of a competition investigation and subsequent legal proceedings by the Australian Competition and Consumer Commission for misleading consumers[345].

Discrimination by Algorithm

Of course the flip side to the beneficent "*micro-targeting*" practices we discuss above is the potential for algorithms to facilitate unlawful discrimination against consumers, to potentially exclude consumers or deprive them from optimal pricing, or other digitally provided services whether directly and overtly or inadvertently. This concept is discussed at length in Chapter Nine on bias.

Self-Preferencing

Self-preferencing refers to the exclusionary and/or self-benefiting techniques adopted by the so-called "*walled garden*" markets we discuss above to favour their own products at the expense of competitive ones from third parties. The *Google Shopping* case[346] is an extreme case illustrating the practice. By selective application of its own ranking

---

344 a particular example of this would be the way in which Amazon hides its "account closure" function, burying it in an obscure part of the website (not related to the "my account" section) taking seven embedded website clicks to reach, followed by an automated webchat – See *How Dark Patterns Trick You Online*, YouTube video by Nerdwriter1

345 The ACCC's complaints were upheld by the Australian Federal Court in *ACCC v Trivago N.V. [2020] FCA 16* (20 January 2020)

346 EU Case AT.39740, 27th June 2017

algorithms, Google was found to have given its own comparison shopping service preferential treatment over competitor services in its general search results pages and consequently to have infringed EU competition law.

Generative AI

As noted elsewhere in this book, Generative AI systems have made a seismic impact across society and have the potential to completely recast commercial markets across an entire landscape of sectors: having not just a direct impact on the provision of technology related services but also indirectly on others.

We have yet to fully grasp how these changes will manifest in competition law terms but there is now doubt that whilst the technology may improve market access in some cases, it is likely to amplify the anti-competitive effects discussed elsewhere in this chapter.

Regulatory Responses

Competition and anti-trust law has a long history both in Europe and the United States – certainly reaching back before the advent of digital computers.

Some argue that Competition authorities are increasingly becoming less capable of taking on anti-competitive behaviours which will ultimately harm consumers because economic activity is transitioning away from the human physical medium towards a digital environment which takes place within and between autonomous machines. We have already examined the potential duality of impact of these technologies in relation to competition and anti-trust principles, which inevitably is highly dependent on context.

What to date then has the response been of the Competition authorities to the use of these technologies?

There is increasing evidence that regulators have developed and deepened their understanding of anti-competitive machine learning led behaviours and are themselves approaching these issues with higher degrees of sophistication. I wrote in 2018 on an OECD consultation document that was published in mid-2017 on the threats posed by algorithmic collusion[347], and the responses of various international regulators which were less than insightful. Since then, the UK Competition and Markets Authority taken an increasingly proactive approach to the technology – it ran a consultation on Algorithmic Harm in 2021[348] and is now, following the introduction of the UK government's AI Governance White Paper[349], and in light of the impact of Generative AI discussed above, conducting an initial review of Foundation Models which we discuss in more detail in Chapter Fourteen[350].

In the US, the FTC has shown an increasingly proactive willingness to involve itself in wide-ranging AI policing on a trade and consumer related basis generally, in a similar manner to the privacy and data protection focus adopted by regulators within the EU and UK[351].

The FTC assumes responsibility for this wider role as part of its remit under the Fair Credit Reporting Act (FCRA) 1970 and the Equal Credit Opportunity Act (ECOA) 1974 which both address automated decision making. The FTC Act itself prohibits unfair and deceptive practices causing loss to consumers arising from the use of AI. The FTC's own guidance in this space provides that the use of AI should be transparent,

347 Algorithms and Collusion – Summaries of Contributions, OECD 21-23 June 2017, DAF/COMP/WD(2017) 2

348 Algorithms: How they can reduce competition and harm consumers, 19th January 2021

349 See the UK AI Governance White Paper *A pro-innovation approach to AI regulation, 22 June 2023* https://www.gov.uk/government/publications/ai-regulation-a-pro-innovation-approach/white-paper

350 *AI Foundation Models: Initial Review*, Competition and Markets Authority, 4th May 2023

351 See the discussion in Chapter Seven on the Everalbum case

fair and empirically sound, while fostering accountability.[352]

The position however on officially reported cases remains essentially the same: there has been a paucity of officially reported cases considering the effect of machine learning in a competition scenario. In the US and UK the competition authorities have considered a case where price matching algorithms were used to implement a cartel between Amazon marketplace competitors[353], but no cases have yet been considered where the issue of parallel, algorithm driven pricing has been considered, or where machine learning solutions have "independently" arrived at a cartelised price.

Undoubtedly regulators are live to the issues involved in the use of potentially autonomous agents in a competition context – the big question for the immediate and near-term future is the extent to which they will be able to identify anti-competitive behaviours and enforce them within existing competition law frameworks.

352 See *Using Artificial Intelligence and Algorithms* https://www.ftc.gov/news-events/blogs/business-blog/2020/04/using-artificial-intelligence-algorithms

353 See U.S. v. Topkins, 2015 and CMA case 2015 n. 50223

CHAPTER TWELVE

AUTOMATION AND AI SERVICE PROVISION

In this chapter we focus on the evolution of third-party AI service provision. The machine learning and AI market is increasingly moving in this direction: away from bespoke systems created by businesses and towards commoditised 'off the shelf' machine learning based service offers – in much the same way as the ERP (enterprise resource planning) and CRM (customer relationship management) markets have evolved over the last twenty or so years[354].

Robotic Process Outsourcing

Robotic process outsourcing, or robotic process automation ("**RPO**") is not a new concept – it refers to the deployment of automation, whether that be robots or other machines, to replace humans in task-based processes. Typically, RPOs have a hybrid characteristic in that they tend to deliver managed services through a combination of human workers with an automated element.

Industries such as manufacturing have been using progressively complex degrees of automation since the time of the industrial revolution in the early 19th century. Robotic assembly of motor vehicles was pioneered in the mid to late 1960s with the use of spot welding robots by General Motors, quickly followed by more flexible and microprocessor-controlled units in the mid-1970s. By the mid-1980s the industry had been transformed.

[354] Whereas once this was the domain of bespoke developers, these markets are now dominated by global companies SAP and Oracle

What machine learning brings to robotic process outsourcing is the ability for robots to assume significantly more complex tasks to those that have previously been undertaken. To continue the car manufacturing analogy, many such robots are now semi-autonomous, with degrees of environment processing, enabling flexible interaction with a changing environment that are at least equivalent to the autonomous vehicles currently being launched on the driving market.

We should not however confine our perspective to manufacturing. Machine learning is opening markets to RPO that have hitherto only been able to be automated on a limited basis, such as the provision of semi-professional tasks involving a high degree of human interaction – front office skills such as call centre and helpdesk operatives for example. The prediction is that ultimately professional level skills will be open to automation, such as those currently practiced by lawyers and accountants.

There are real and complex political and moral arguments at play with ever increasing waves of automation replacing human workers, and the workplace is under a degree of existential threat in the mid to near future the likes of which have not been seen since the industrial revolution. This is a book however about the practical legal consequences of the deployment of such technology. In this sense, outside the other issues that we have analysed in this book, these disruptive considerations are no more different (or at least equivalent to) the considerations that have to be managed when outsourcing in the traditional sense.

Conventional outsourcing, for the uninitiated, entails the transfer of an internally managed service or operation to an external service provider. When introducing automation and artificial intelligence into the workplace, what therefore are the primary practical legal consequences that need to be borne in mind? The first and by far away the most significant consideration is the management of workforce displacement.

Typically in a conventional outsourcing carried out within the UK (and indeed the wider EU), when a service is outsourced, the rights embodied in the EU's Transfers of Undertakings Directive[355] and enacted in the UK under the Transfer of Undertakings (Protection of Employment) Regulations 2006[356]. Broadly speaking, this stipulates that (unlike many jurisdictions where employment is "*at will*", such as the United States), when an "*undertaking*"[357] is transferred from customer to service provider (a "*relevant transfer*"), the employment of those employees carrying out the service immediately prior to the transfer is carried over to the service provider, without any break in continuity, thus preserving their extant employment rights. This means that the service provider must continue their employment on equivalent terms. Any dismissals carried out because of a relevant transfer are deemed to be unfair unless there is an *economic*, *technical* or *organisational* reason for the dismissals which for the purposes of the legislation[358] are deemed to justified. In such circumstances, the affected employee is considered to be redundant and may be entitled to statutory compensation if they have been employed for a continuous period of more than two years[359].

Plainly in the case of robotic displacement, there is no transfer of undertaking, no continuity of employment and redundancy or redeployment of the affected employees is the only option available to the employer. The Employment Rights Act provides as follows: "*For the purposes of this Act an employee who is dismissed shall be taken to be dismissed by reason of redundancy if the dismissal is wholly or mainly attributable to— (a) the fact that his employer has ceased or intends to cease—(i) to carry on the business for the purposes of which the employee was employed by him, or (ii) to carry on that business in the place where the employee was so employed,*

---

355 2001/23/EC

356 SI 2006/246

357 There is much UK and EU law on what constitutes an undertaking, but essentially this is the business operation engaged in economic activities which is to be transferred to the service provider, see further *Höfner & Elser v. Macrotron GmbH [1991] ECR I-1979*

358 See the Employment Rights Act 1996, s98(2)(c)

359 s135 Employment Rights Act 1996

or (b) the fact that the requirements of that business—(i) for employees to carry out work of a particular kind, or (ii) for employees to carry out work of a particular kind in the place where the employee was employed by the employer, have ceased or diminished or are expected to cease or diminish."[360]. The Act continues with the following embellishment: "*In subsection (1) "cease" and "diminish" mean cease and diminish either permanently or temporarily and for whatever reason.*"[361].

Somewhat perversely this does mean that in terms of justifying grounds for redundancy, the law makes it demonstrably easier to do so in circumstances where a machine is to replace a person.

Whether this will ultimately lead to a public policy change in the event of widespread displacement remains to be seen – already there has been some debate in the UK and the USA about the introduction of a "*workplace automation*" tax, to help fund the retraining of displaced employees. South Korea has taken the first tentative steps on this path by implementing an indirect tax on workplace automation by applying in effect a reduced tax incentive benefit to workplaces originally designed to boost productivity[362]. Somewhat more radically, some economists have suggested going further and have advocated the introduction of a universal basic income as a solution to the inequality and inevitable work displacement caused by the emergence of robots and artificial intelligence[363].

Outside of workplace displacement, what are the other problematic issues which will need to be resolved when outsourcing to artificial intelligence?

---

360 s139(1) Employment Rights Act 1996

361 s139(6) Employment Rights Act 1996

362 See http://www.koreatimes.co.kr/www/news/tech/2017/08/133_234312.html "*Korea takes first step to introduce 'Robot Tax*"

363 The suggestion was made by professor Sir Christopher Pissarides, a Nobel laureate and the Regius professor at the London School of Economics during the World Economic Forum in Davos, 20th January 2016

Many of these will revolve around the nature of the task and duties which have been delegated. As has been apparent throughout previous chapters of this book – there are going to be specific duties and responsibilities which cannot yet be transferred to a machine learning system because the law has not yet developed a coherent theory of artificial *personhood*. This is likely to be a hugely important step if we are to confer onto machines the responsibility to make decisions which have real (ie. legal and moral) consequences for human beings. Unless and until the law evolves in this way (currently not the direction of travel[364]), ultimately what can be outsourced will necessarily be constrained, and we will be left with activities and tasks that are not (or are at least, minimally) regulated.

Aside from these considerations, outsourcing agreements contain a variety of supplier focussed contractual obligations and liabilities to be managed which in theory could be extended to artificially intelligent systems – although some thought would need to be given to their application. Many of the areas which are likely to be applicable have already been discussed at length elsewhere in this book. These include the compliance issues around big data analytics (see the commentary in Chapter Six) and the protection and management of intellectual property, both in relation to deliverables created by the machine learning system in the course of the provision of the outsourced services (which as we discussed previously would likely be covered, certainly in the UK by the machine generated copyright provisions of the Copyright, Designs and Patents Act 1988[365]) and in respect of the machine learning system itself (again, see the commentary in Chapter Eight). Consideration would also need to be given to ongoing service management and Service Level agreements (or SLAs) as these are a feature of most traditional outsourcing agreements. As the name implies, these enforce mandated levels of service performance upon suppliers to ensure that the services

[364] See the debate on artificial personhood in Chapter Four and the discussions in Chapters Five (on the EU Artificial Intelligence Act) and Fourteen (on regulatory responses)

[365] See s178 of the CDPA 1988 and s9(3) respectively

being performed do not drop below a particular standard. Whereas in traditional outsourcing agreements these typically are focussed on *direct performance by the supplier of the services*, there is an increasing trend in complex RPOs for these to translate to *maintenance and support of the AI system performing the service*, as these are typically the non-AI (human based) services which are performed in an RPO context and which can be enforced in a traditional manner. Interestingly, in terms of SLA and contract enforcement in RPO there is a potential role to play here for another upcoming technology, so called block-chain enabled "*smart contract*" systems. Initiatives such as the Accord Project[366] an international working party made up of several law firms and technology businesses are looking to develop open-source technology standards to transition contracts from static documents into fully integrated components of commercial systems – which would mean for example – automatic deduction or "netting off" of service credits in the event that a particular service level was not met, without human intervention.

Artificial Intelligence as a Service (AIaaS)

One of the biggest blocks to date to small and medium sized enterprise in the deployment of machine learning systems and tools has been the level of investment and expertise that is required to successfully build and train such systems. Unsurprisingly this requires a degree of specialist skill that is beyond the means of most in the SME sector and possibly even some larger businesses – it is also in many cases, "*non-core*" in terms of business objectives.

Coupled with this has been a strong trend in the outsourcing market, driven by ubiquity in cloud computing, to move away from traditional "*on premise*" solutions to service based "*on demand*" SaaS (Software as a Service) solutions or Cloud based architecture for the delivery of complex managed services.

As machine learning systems become ever more complex and capable we

---

366 See https://www.accordproject.org/

are seeing in turn a complex re-imagining and commoditisation of service delivery related tools and products and the emergence of artificial intelligence as a service or "AIaaS". What AIaaS attempts to offer is a commoditised cognitive computing platform, delivered via the cloud, that allows businesses to leverage the power of pre-built and trained machine learning solutions, either directly, or as part of a robotic process outsourcing via a third party.

AIaaS solutions are broadly speaking structured either as data, compute or pre-packaged services. AIaaS data solutions provide the convenience of ready-made pools of data to enable fast and effective training of machine learning models for common or generic problems – these might for example be comprised of masses of facial images for facial recognition applications. Compute services enable common infrastructural computing tasks to be carried out that are closely integrated with machine learning solutions – such as batch processing. Pre-packaged AIaaS allows for the provision of ready-made AI applications on demand that can be integrated into enterprise offerings.

Use of AIaaS solutions, whether pre-packaged or via data or compute models clearly brings convenience and speed of implementation to many "standard" machine learning solutions, such as facial recognition, language translation or natural language processing. However from a legal perspective such solutions introduce additional levels of difficulty to what may already be a significantly complex RPO arrangement. Numerous issues spring to mind – as a licensee of AIaaS data services you will need to be able to seek sufficient reassurance that the pools of training data that may be provided by the platform provider are sufficiently curated to avoid bias but have not been overfitted. Equally speaking, if you are seeking to include a commoditised application to support a facial recognition application, you will need to have specific assurance that the application has been adequately trained. Disclosure levels and transparency are likely to be key determinants for the customers of AIaaS providers, but equally speaking will prove to be a very difficult interface for the platform providers themselves to navigate, who will be naturally incentivised to keep as much confidential as possible, for fear of giving away valuable proprietary information.

Complex decision-making machine learning systems are likely to be harder to manage from a liability perspective if they are dependent upon AIaaS offerings, whether or not they form part of an RPO. Generally speaking, that is because in the event of a contract default – or even circumstances where you need to be able to justify or explain the consequences of a particular decision to an external third party, such as a regulator, you will be faced with having to work back through the licence terms granting access to the AIaaS platform. You will then have to determine the extent to which the provider of the AIaaS cognitive computing platform itself (with all the inherent difficulties we have already discussed in terms of "*black boxes*" and causation) is willing or able to provide an explanation or demonstrate that it is not the cause of the relevant default[367] – not of itself a trivial problem[368].

As I noted above, AIaaS platforms that are used in this way tend to be heavily proprietary and confidential, and the services they offer are often provided on a "*take it or leave it basis*". As such it seems unlikely that you will be able to open the lid of the black box and peer inside should something unexpected occur. In fact the licences granted in such circumstances are typically drafted defensively to protect the platform provider.

I would add as a final caveat that we are in the early stages of the evolution of such services. It seems likely that such large platform providers may have to provide a *de minimis* level of transparency in order to establish credibility in their service offers and also to justify their compliance with law and use in regulated contexts.

---

[367] The new EU AI Liability Directive will make proof of causation in AI related cases easier to establish in the European Union by way of its 'rebuttable presumption of causality' (Article 4 AILD). See discussion in Chapters Four and Five

[368] Recall the refusal of Equivant, developers of COMPAS, a parole evaluation system, to release details of its internal operations. See Chapter Ten

MLOps

Whereas AIaaS describes the delivery of artificial intelligence by a third party to an enterprise customer, MLOps can be distinguished as the practice of embedding commoditised enterprise AI within such customers.

MLOps is a relatively new discipline and is based on the existing DevOps process of integrating IT (that is to say the process of deploying, running, and sometimes writing, applications) within an enterprise[369].

Many businesses now have the capability to leverage "self-serve" AI tools, such as pre-configured models and datasets from open-source hosts such as Github and the Linux Foundation in order to create tailored AI tools.

MLOps in essence is a production lifecycle focussed on the granular activities and methodology involved in a successful machine learning integration.

Businesses that adopt MLOps can rapidly, frequently and reliably build test and release machine learning into production on an operationalised basis. This might include standardising activities such as data collection, data ingestion, analysis and curation; and validating data and labelling data, as well as model training and model evaluation, eventually leading to full machine learning system deployment[370]. Seldon Core is an example of an open-source enterprise platform which makes use of MLOps for rapid deployment of machine learning models[371]. It utilises Kubernetes (essentially an open-source containerised orchestration system)[372] for automated application deployment.

---

369 See *What is MLOps?* https://blogs.nvidia.com/blog/2020/09/03/what-is-mlops/

370 Ibid., note 12

371 See www.seldon.io

372 Kubernetes or K8s was named after the Greek word for the helmsman of a ship or pilot and was developed by Google Native Cloud Foundation

Any analysis of MLOps from a legal risk perspective is likely to be highly dependent on the circumstances of a particular deployment. As the process is closely aligned to (if not exclusively) the use of open-source models and data, standard intellectual property open-source considerations will apply in relation to the extent to which subsequent use and exploitation of AI tools developed in this way may be restricted (for example there is likely to be a difference in treatment between AI tools developed for 'in house' use as opposed to those which are intended to be sold on as commercial products). As such a detailed understanding of the underlying open-source licence type is likely to be essential.

CHAPTER THIRTEEN

ARTIFICIAL INTELLIGENCE AND CORPORATE LAW

In this chapter on Corporate law we take a closer look at the extent to which machine learning solutions are taking over human duties, both inside and outside the boardroom, whether by direct appointment as directors, or as delegates of the duties owed by directors to their companies and shareholders.

The cybernetic corporation

Before we look more closely at directors and their duties however, it is worth sketching a picture of the holy grail of automation in a corporate context (or nightmare depending upon your point of view). This is of course the fully cybernetic corporation. A cybernetic corporation is essentially a corporate machine – where all of the duties of the directors and employees are subsumed and taken over by artificial intelligence and robots undertake all necessary interaction with the physical world – such as fulfilment, logistics and call centre management. Decentralised Autonomous Organisations or DAOs take the concept one stage further and apply blockchain verification technologies to the decisions of such corporatized machines[373].

Clearly this is the stuff of science fiction and we are not yet at a stage where these entities can sustainably exist (other than in terms of early

[373] The original DAO was an investor directed venture capital fund which launched in April 2016 and became defunct in September 2016. The code of the DAO was open-source. It had no conventional management structure or board of directors, was instantiated on the Ethereum blockchain and was effectively stateless. See *Experiments in Algorithmic Governance: A History and ethnography of 'the DAO' a failed Decentralized Autonomous Organisation*, Quinn DuPont, Univ. Toronto

experimentation) – however there are signs that machine learning is beginning to encroach into corporate governance.

Appointment of artificial intelligence systems as company directors

There are already reports of artificial intelligence systems being "appointed" to boards, either as directors or as observers. In 2016 for example the Nordic financial services company Tieto Corporation appointed the AI *Alicia T*, as "*a member of its leadership team*" and became the first company in Europe to do so. Tieto however was preceded by Deep Knowledge Ventures in Hong Kong who had in 2014 appointed an AI named *Vital* (Validating Investment Tool for Advancing Life Sciences) as an "*observer*" over their board of directors.

What then is the current status of artificial intelligence in the boardroom? Could machine learning systems be conceivably appointed as directors?

So far as the law of England and Wales is concerned this question is governed by the Companies Act 2006 rather inconclusively, which provides that "*(1) a private company must have at least one director. (2) a public company must have at least two directors.*"[374] and "*(1) a company must have at least one director who is a natural person. (2) this requirement is met if the office of director is held by a natural person as a corporation sole or otherwise by virtue of an office*"[375].

Whilst not explicitly provided for it is evident from its subsequent provisions that the Companies Act only contemplates the appointment of natural and legal persons (ie bodies corporate) as directors. This is because sections 163 and 164 respectively only describe the particulars of natural and legal persons that need to be entered into the company's register of directors.

It appears that so far as AI is concerned, machine learning systems will

[374] Section 154 of the Companies Act 2006

[375] Section 155 of the Companies Act 2006

not (at least in the UK) be entitled to be directly appointed as directors. This is because, as we have previously considered in other contexts, no theory of *artificial personhood* equivalent to legal personality for corporations has yet been developed to confer upon them legal status (for more on this, please see Chapter Four under the heading entitled "*Individuation or Artificial Personhood*").

The next question to consider in terms of immediate impact in the boardroom is the extent to which the use of machine learning in a corporate governance context is permitted when one takes into account the fiduciary and statutory duties which are owed by directors to the boards of the companies they are appointed to.

Delegation

Before we discuss the duties themselves, it is probably worth looking briefly at the extent to which directors can delegate those duties – as this will be of immediate relevance to our discussion. Table A (the model form of articles of association prescribed under UK companies legislation[376]) allows directors the ability to delegate their duties as follows: " *(1) Subject to the articles, the directors may delegate any of the powers which are conferred on them under the articles— (a) to such person or committee; (b) by such means (including by power of attorney); (c) to such an extent; (d) in relation to such matters or territories; and (e) on such terms and conditions; as they think fit. (2) If the directors so specify, any such delegation may authorise further delegation of the directors' powers by any person to whom they are delegated. (3) The directors may revoke any delegation in whole or part, or alter its terms and conditions*"[377]. It seems apparent then that so far as delegation is concerned, the law simply does not contemplate these duties being taken over by anything other than a legal or natural person or committee. We are effectively in the same position we discussed earlier in the context of the direct appointment of

376 See the Companies (Model Articles) Regulations 2008

377 See article 5 of the Model Articles for companies limited by shares

AIs as directors. Unless there is an evolution to grant some form of artificial personhood to machine learning solutions, this will not be possible. This does not prevent of course artificial intelligence being used in the context of corporate governance – merely that if it is used, the legal basis will have little more significance than if a director used an ordinary computer in the context of his or her duties – AI in essence in this sense becomes transparent and is relegated to a tool or instrumental extension to be utilised. The individual director remains, in these circumstances, fully accountable and responsible for his or her acts.

Director's general duties

So far as the duties themselves are concerned, the Companies Act sets out several key "general" duties – as previously stated in different contexts, I don't propose to list them all here, but rather to concentrate on the ones which may be potentially significant in relation to the use of machine learning. These are the three general duties which are relevant – to *promote the success of the company* (to behave in a way most likely to promote the success of the company)[378]; to *exercise independent judgment*[379]; and to *exercise reasonable care, skill and diligence*[380].

Evidently there is already sufficient anecdotal evidence in the market to suggest that the effective deployment of machine learning solutions in the enterprise can have very beneficial effects in terms of optimising performance and efficiency.

As use of machine learning becomes more and more widespread and such systems become more and more capable it seems likely that the need for directors to advocate the use of such tools within their corporations in order to *promote the success of the company* is likely to grow and that this duty will become commensurately stronger. What is interesting however

378 Section 172 Companies Act 2006

379 Section 173 Companies Act 2006

380 Section 174 Companies Act 2006

is that in large part much of the usefulness of machine learning solutions lies in their ability to predict or to provide real-time analysis in relation to a particular situation – in short a *judgmental view*, and potentially the ability to do this more accurately than any human being. It would seem therefore that this has the very real potential to conflict with the other duty I have called out above, the need to *exercise independent judgment*. This duty was originally created to prevent bias or narrow partisanship on the part of a director and his or her decisions – being beholden to one stakeholder or interest or their appointing shareholder at the expense of all others was unlikely to further the overarching interests of the company in a good sense – but equally speaking one can see how blind adherence to the decisions of a machine learning system, without necessarily exercising a critical review or promoting an alternative approach could also cause a director to fall into the same trap.

There is of course, a similar tautology in relation to the last of the director's duties that we discuss in this chapter – that of *exercising reasonable skill, care and diligence*. Again one can see how the duty might promote increased use of artificial intelligence in the boardroom if it leads to more efficient, rounded and evaluated decisions – in effect enhancing skill and diligence. Misapplied however, it might lead to a completely contrary result and ultimately breach of that duty. As in previous discussions in this book, context, use and application are critical to the successful deployment and utilisation of AI.

Transactional considerations – automated due diligence

Corporate transactions are of course an important feature of this legal landscape – companies and ownership are not static and invariably they will be subject to mergers, acquisitions, divestments and re-organisations. Machine learning has a role to play in this environment as well – principally around one of the key activities involved in any such deal – the corporate due diligence exercise. Typically this involves a detailed analysis and investigation of all of the debts, liabilities and assets of the corporate entity that is either being sold, purchased or merged – usually the exercise is split into three different parts – *financial* which focusses on verifying the financial information provided by the counterparty and to assess the underlying performance of the business; *commercial* which considers the market in which the target business sits and the potential competitive landscape; and *legal* which considers all of the legal elements of the transaction. This might cover for example the contracts that the business holds from customers; employment contracts with key employees; real property documentation such as leases; critical supply agreements into the business; how any intellectual property assets might be held and any actual or pending litigation.

Machine learning solutions are becoming more ubiquitous in relation to financial and legal due diligence exercises, leading many journalists of hyperbolic predisposition to prematurely predict the end of either lawyers or accountants or both. What these solutions do is ingest and filter the relevant financial or legal information on an automated basis into a pre-structured due diligence report. Typically this avoids the need for armies of junior lawyers or accountants to review the information manually to produce the same digest[381].

Generally speaking, automating the due diligence process also allows for significant increases in speed (machine learning solutions tend to be quicker than human beings) and decreases in cost (machine learning solutions are not paid by the hour as are legal or financial professionals but are subject to a licensing fee which tends to be much lower). There are therefore significant and apparent business benefits to introducing these processes into corporate transactions – I would however strike a note of caution and ask you the reader to cast your mind back to the contents of Chapters One and Three. All machine learning based artificial intelligence requires significant and competent training in order to achieve good results. If the automated due diligence system that is deployed in a particular transaction has not been trained properly then the result it produces will at best be poor and at worst plain wrong. This

381 Market leading solutions include the diligence platforms provided by Luminance – see www.luminance.com and Kira – see www.kirasystems.com

is now compounded by the issues created by Generative AI systems, in particular a pre-disposition in some systems to invent content or to "hallucinate" in relation to outputs[382], which can have very real consequences in liability terms for practitioners (and enterprises) seeking to rely on such outputs. Given the professional duties that are owed by both accountancy firms and law firms to their clients – and in particular to act in the client's best interests, and also the potential for clients to initiate professional misconduct proceedings, it would seem sensible as a basic minimum to ensure that proper steps have been taken to verify that any machine learning system which is used has been properly tested and trained (and its outputs appropriately verified). In many cases it may actually be sensible for the professional advisor to go one step further and double check the actual automated due diligence report produced (which may perversely completely undermine the business rationales of speed and cost discussed earlier). I would suggest that the worst course of conduct is to accept any such report "*in blind faith*".

[382] See the discussion in Chapter Three

CHAPTER FOURTEEN

POLITICAL, REGULATORY AND INDUSTRY RESPONSES

As I mentioned right back in Chapter One, and to some degree predicted in the last edition of this book, the degree and extent of regulation (or at least proposed regulation) of artificial intelligence and machine learning technologies has moved forward significantly – the most notable example being the draft EU Artificial Intelligence Act, which now has its own chapter. There are however significant developments elsewhere which also deserve some discussion.

Please bear in mind that much of this discussion is ongoing within the relevant organisations and or governmental regulators, so will be subject to change and adaptation. This discussion is also limited to those initiatives which are deemed to be of sufficient significance to merit a mention – it is not by any means a complete and exhaustive exposition[383].

I would hope however that many initiatives are sufficiently matured to enable a perspective on where the ultimate regulatory destination will be. With that in mind, there are a number of initiatives that are worth mentioning, as they reflect well some of the issues and concerns raised in this book.

---

383 For a more detailed analysis of global AI regulation, see *Artificial Intelligence: Law Over Borders Comparative Guide*, published by the Global Legal Post

Industry Initiatives

The Partnership on AI

The first, and possibly the most significant is the Partnership on AI or "PAI"[384] which has been established between Google, Microsoft, Apple, Amazon, IBM and Meta (together with a number of other leading industry participants).

The PAI attempts broadly to ensure that industry leaders in the development of AI do so on an ethical basis, taking into account a number of thematic "pillars" or priorities. These pillars include establishing conventions for safety in the use of AI and robotic systems (a key element of which is ensuring that AI systems cede gracefully when they fail rather than putting the user in a catastrophic position); making AI fair, transparent and accountable (in order to increase the auditability of decisions taken by AI systems); promoting co-operative AI systems; examining the way in which AI will influence the distribution of jobs and the nature of work – with a view to minimising disruption; investigating augmented systems that work collaboratively between humans and AI and variously considering the extent to which AI will influence society to ensure that it is for the greater good[385]. Members of the Partnership on AI also commit to uphold a set of eight tenets which attempt to define the way in which they approach the development and use of the technology[386]. These tenets aspirationally set admirable goals, however it

384 See www.partnershiponai.org

385 See https://partnershiponai.org/about/

386 The tenets are extracted at https://partnershiponai.org/tenets/ and can be summarised as follows 1) seeking to ensure that AI benefits and empowers as many people as possible 2) educating and listening to the public and engaging stakeholders 3) committing to open research and dialogue on ethical, social, economic and legal implications of AI 4) making R&D accountable 5) ensuring that domain specific concerns are addressed 6) addressing the challenges of AI by working to protect privacy; understanding all interests; making R&D socially responsible; making sure the technology is robust, reliable & trustworthy; and opposing use and development which would violate human rights 7) making AI understandable and interpretable and 8) striving to create a culture of co-operation

remains to be seen how the members will apply these in practice.

OpenAI

Since the last edition of this book, OpenAI, initially set up as a non-profit AI research company focussed on developing AGI or artificial general intelligence, has controversially become a fully and overtly commercial enterprise.

Originally set up to counteract the concentrative effect of big corporation re-search into AI technologies and to ensure that AGI would be developed to ultimately benefit all of humanity, OpenAI was founded in 2015 jointly by entrepreneurs Sam Altman and Elon Musk. It has been at the forefront of generative AI development and is responsible for launching large language model Chat-GPT as well as the generative image model, Dall-E.

The pivot by OpenAI into overtly commercial enterprise and away from its original tenets, which were to counteract the concentrative effect of big corporation research into AI technologies has caused Elon Musk to openly disavow his connection with the organisation[387].

Political and Regulatory Initiatives

The EU

The proposed new Artificial Intelligence Act and its accompanying measure, the AI Liability Directive, are discussed at length in Chapter Five, so I do not propose to discuss those initiatives here.

---

trust and openness amongst AI scientists

387 See *Elon Musk just disowned ChatGPT parent company OpenAI* see: https://fortune.com/2023/02/17/chatgpt-elon-musk-openai-microsoft-company-regulator-oversight/

The UK

Draft AI Governance White Paper

Since the publication of the last edition of this book, the UK government has published its much vaunted (and somewhat delayed) AI Governance White Paper[388]. Rather than adopt a 'top down' unitary approach in the manner of the EU Artificial Intelligence Act, the UK has chosen to take a more sector led approach.

This sector led approach is designed to balance the need for innovation with clarity in terms of regulatory approach, and stems from concerns that the EU Artificial Intelligence Act regime may prove too inflexible and stultify investment in the industry. In the words of the UK Government: "*Responding to risk and building public trust are important drivers for regulation. But clear and consistent regulation can also support business investment and build confidence in innovation. Throughout our extensive engagement, industry repeatedly emphasised that consumer trust is key to the success of innovation economies. We therefore need a clear, proportionate approach to regulation that enables the responsible application of AI to flourish. Instead of creating cumbersome rules applying to all AI technologies, our framework ensures that regulatory measures are proportionate to context and outcomes, by focusing on the use of AI rather than the technology itself.*"[389]

The paper sets out that regulators will be tasked with developing regimes which are directed on the outcomes AI could generate in applications which relate to their particular sectors[390].

---

388 See *A pro-innovation approach to AI regulation, 22 June 2023* https://www.gov.uk/government/publications/ai-regulation-a-pro-innovation-approach/white-paper

389 See UK Government AI Governance White Paper (note 5), paragraph 6 of the Executive Summary.

390 See Section 3.2.2, paragraph 45 of the UK AI Governance White Paper

The sector led approach is underpinned by five principles which readers of the Ethics primer in Chapter Two will find broadly familiar[391]. These can be broadly summarised as follows:

- *Safety, security and robustness*

  AI Systems should function in a robust, secure and safe wat throughout the AI lifecycle.

  Regulators may need to introduce measures to ensure that AI systems are technically secure and function reliably as intended.

  When applying this principle, regulators will need to consider providing guidance which is co-ordinated and coherent with other regulators.

- *Appropriate transparency and explainability*

  AI systems should be appropriately transparent and explainable.

  Transparency is defined in the AI Governance White Paper as the Communication of information about an AI system (such as information on how, when and for which purposes a system may be used), explainability looks to the decision-making process of the AI system itself.

  Regulators will need to have sufficient information about AI systems and their associated inputs and outputs to define the application of the other principles. They should support and encourage system lifecycle actors to implement appropriate transparency measures.

  The principle acknowledges that the current *state of the art* does not allow sufficient explainability and as such remains an

[391] See Section 3.2.3, paragraph 52

important research and development challenge.

- *Fairness*

  AI systems should not undermine the legal rights of individuals or organisations, discriminate unfairly or create unfair market outcomes.

  Regulators may need to develop and publish descriptions and illustrations of fairness that apply to AI systems used within their regulatory domains. They will need to be able to describe what fairness means within their sector in order to ensure a proportionate and context-specific approach.

  In particular the paper provides that this principle should be applied consistently with the Equality Act 2010, the GDPR, consumer and competition law and relevant sector-based fairness rules.

- *Accountability and governance*

  Governance measures should be in place to ensure effective oversight of the supply and use of AI systems.

  Regulators should look for ways to ensure that clear expectations for regulatory compliance and good practice are placed on appropriate actors in the AI supply chain, as well as encouraging the use of governance procedures that ensure those expectations are met.

  The concept of assurance techniques such as impact assessments should be used to identify potential risks early in the development lifecycle of a relevant AI system, and proper accountability should be demonstrated by providing documentation on key decisions as well as allowing audits.

- *Contestability and redress*

  Users and impacted third parties in the AI lifecycle should be able to contest an AI decision or outcome that is harmful or creates a material risk of harm.

  Regulators will be expected to clarify existing routes to contestability and redress.

The initial approach proposed by the UK Government is non-statutory[392], however following a period of implementation, the government reserves the right to impose a new statutory duty on regulators to require them to have due regard to the principles (as well as to introduce broader statutory measures).

Clearly the flipside of putting in place such a flexible decentralised framework is there is a risk of incoherence and disorganisation as between regulators. This is acknowledged by the UK Government which also proposes the creation of central co-ordinating functions[393] and oversight in what is termed a "*central risk function*".

It is currently unclear from the contents of the AI Governance White Paper as to what organisation will exercise these proposed central risk functions (or whether indeed a new "super regulator" will be created to exercise such oversight). At the outset it is likely that central government itself will be responsible for this role.

The UK's AI Governance White Paper also acknowledges the transformative impact of foundation models on society[394], however other than emphasising the flexibility of the proposed regulatory framework and the need to keep the UK in the forefront of generative AI development, it stops short of definitively setting out a roadmap for

[392] See section 3.2.4, paragraphs 55-59

[393] See section 3.3.1 for details of the proposed oversight functions

[394] See section 3.3.3

dealing with these models.

This has led to some criticism that the UK is placing innovation and investment ahead of safety concerns in relation to generative AI systems, particularly as the AI White Paper was published on the same day as a letter from several global experts on AI, calling for a pause in the development of foundation models[395].

UK CMA Initial Review on Foundation Models

As noted earlier in Chapter Eleven, the UK Competition and Markets Authority has commenced an initial review into the market impact of foundation models. This is stated to be in line with and consistent with the UK's AI Governance White Paper[396].

The CMA's remit for this initial review is to examine the following themes:

- *Competition and barriers to entry in the development of foundation models;*
- *the impact foundation models may have on competition in other markets; and*
- *Consumer protection*

Its findings are expected to be published in early September 2023.

[395] See *UK at odds with Elon Musk and other experts on AI regulation* Tech Monitor, March 29, 2023 https://techmonitor.ai/technology/ai-and-automation/ai-regulation-uk-elon-musk

[396] See *AI Foundation Models: Initial Review*, CMA 23rd May 2023, foreword

The United States

The draft Algorithmic Accountability Act

In the United States, attempts have been made to introduce a federal measure to regulate AI decision making in some serious contexts, the so-called Algorithmic Accountability Act of 2022[397]. It was introduced as an attempt to redress an imbalance between large corporations using such technologies and individuals who could potentially be harmed by the use of flawed automated decision-making systems.

The Act proposes that direct oversight powers are conferred on the US Federal Trade Commission. It would require companies to gauge (by way of impact assessment) the impacts of automated decision systems they use or sell that undertake what is termed an "*augmented critical decision process*".

In general it empowers the FTC to create regulations for such assessment and reporting, and mandates annual anonymised reporting as well as provide a central evidential repository of information where individuals can review which critical decisions have been automated by which companies.

As at the time of writing, this measure is sitting at Committee stage in the House of Representatives and it is unclear whether it will garner enough bipartisan support to progress further.

Blueprint for an AI Bill of Rights

In October 2022, the Biden Presidency's Office of Science and Technology Policy published a blueprint for an AI Bill of Rights, which set out a non-binding 'best practice' roadmap for AI usage[398].

---

397 See H.R 6850, 117th Congress https://www.congress.gov/bill/117th-congress/house-bill/6580/text

398 See *Blueprint for an AI Bill of Rights: Making Automated Systems Work for the*

The blueprint is essentially an advisory document[399] that is conceptually remarkably similar in approach to the UK's AI Governance White Paper, in that it is founded on a set of core AI ethical principles and extrapolates aspirational behaviours from these. In the case of the blueprint, these are:

- *Safe and effective systems;*
- *algorithmic discrimination protections;*
- *data privacy;*
- *notice and explanation; and*
- *human alternatives, consideration and fallback*

The blueprint is accompanied by a technical companion document which sets out guidance on how to embed these principles from the design and conceptualisation stage, through to usage.

Canada

Artificial Intelligence and Data Act

Canada is also taking steps to legislate in this space and has now published its Artificial Intelligence and Data Act, or AIDA[400].

AIDA was tabled by the Canadian Government as part of Bill C-27, its so called Digital Charter Implementation Act 2022, a consolidating law bringing together several measures, in June 2022. The Canadian law is

---

American People https://www.whitehouse.gov/wp-content/uploads/2022/10/Blueprint-for-an-AI-Bill-of-Rights.pdf

399 Rather bizarrely, it even contains a disclaimer to the effect that it does not constitute official US Government policy.

400 https://ised-isde.canada.ca/site/innovation-better-canada/en/artificial-intelligence-and-data-act-aida-companion-document

overtly designed to align with what are described as evolving international norms in the AI space, including the EU Artificial Intelligence Act, the OECD's AI Principles[401] and the US National Institute of Standards and Technology (NIST) Risk Management Framework[402]. As at the date of writing, the Canadian measure is little more than a 'bare' framework, awaiting a number of key obligations and details[403].

Brazil

Proposed Bill to regulate ethical and responsible use of AI

Brazil has also taken steps to regulate use of AI systems with a new draft law[404]. The draft law, which was introduced to the Brazilian Senate in 2023, proposes an EU style regulatory framework, with various classes of risk based AI, a governance framework which will include the use of algorithmic Impact assessments and a central regulator to oversee compliance throughout Brazil. Unlike the EU Artificial Intelligence Act, the Brazilian measure also includes provisions for civil liability for damages. At the time of writing the final version of the bill is yet to be approved by the Brazilian congress and may undergo further changes.

401 See https://oecd.ai/en/ai-principles

402 See https://csrc.nist.gov/projects/risk-management/about-rmf

403 For an excellent critique of this proposed new Canadian measure, please refer to Barry Sookman's blog on barrysookman.org : *AIDA Companion Document: overview and questions* April 10, 2023 – https://www.barrysookman.com/2023/04/10/aida-companion-document-overview-and-questions/

404 See https://shorturl.at/emrIM

MORE BOOKS BY LAW BRIEF PUBLISHING

A selection of our other titles available now:-

'A Practical Guide to Estate Administration and Crypto Assets' by Richard Marshall
'A Practical Guide to Managing GDPR Data Subject Access Requests – Second Edition' by Patrick O'Kane
'A Practical Guide to Parental Alienation in Private and Public Law Children Cases' by Sam King QC & Frankie Shama
'Contested Heritage – Removing Art from Land and Historic Buildings' by Richard Harwood QC, Catherine Dobson, David Sawtell
'The Limits of Separate Legal Personality: When Those Running a Company Can Be Held Personally Liable for Losses Caused to Third Parties Outside of the Company' by Dr Mike Wilkinson
'A Practical Guide to Transgender Law' by Robin Moira White & Nicola Newbegin
'A Practical Guide to 'Stranded Spouses' in Family Law' by Mani Singh Basi
'A Practical Guide to Residential Freehold Conveyancing' by Lorraine Richardson
'A Practical Guide to Pensions on Divorce for Lawyers' by Bryan Scant
'A Practical Guide to Challenging Sham Marriage Allegations in Immigration Law' by Priya Solanki
'A Practical Guide to Legal Rights in Scotland' by Sarah-Jane Macdonald
'A Practical Guide to New Build Conveyancing' by Paul Sams & Rebecca East
'A Practical Guide to Defending Barristers in Disciplinary Cases' by Marc Beaumont
'A Practical Guide to Inherited Wealth on Divorce' by Hayley Trim
'A Practical Guide to Practice Direction 12J and Domestic Abuse in Private Law Children Proceedings' by Rebecca Cross & Malvika Jaganmohan
'A Practical Guide to Confiscation and Restraint' by Narita Bahra QC, John Carl Townsend, David Winch
'A Practical Guide to the Law of Forests in Scotland' by Philip Buchan
'A Practical Guide to Health and Medical Cases in Immigration Law' by Rebecca Chapman & Miranda Butler

'A Practical Guide to Bad Character Evidence for Criminal Practitioners by Aparna Rao
'A Practical Guide to Extradition Law post-Brexit' by Myles Grandison et al
'A Practical Guide to Hoarding and Mental Health for Housing Lawyers' by Rachel Coyle
'A Practical Guide to Psychiatric Claims in Personal Injury – 2nd Edition' by Liam Ryan
'Stephens on Contractual Indemnities' by Richard Stephens
'A Practical Guide to the EU Succession Regulation' by Richard Frimston
'A Practical Guide to Solicitor and Client Costs – 2nd Edition' by Robin Dunne
'Constructive Dismissal – Practice Pointers and Principles' by Benjimin Burgher
'A Practical Guide to Religion and Belief Discrimination Claims in the Workplace' by Kashif Ali
'A Practical Guide to the Law of Medical Treatment Decisions' by Ben Troke
'Fundamental Dishonesty and QOCS in Personal Injury Proceedings: Law and Practice' by Jake Rowley
'A Practical Guide to the Law in Relation to School Exclusions' by Charlotte Hadfield & Alice de Coverley
'A Practical Guide to Divorce for the Silver Separators' by Karin Walker
'The Right to be Forgotten – The Law and Practical Issues' by Melissa Stock
'A Practical Guide to Planning Law and Rights of Way in National Parks, the Broads and AONBs' by James Maurici QC, James Neill et al
'A Practical Guide to Election Law' by Tom Tabori
'A Practical Guide to the Law in Relation to Surrogacy' by Andrew Powell
'A Practical Guide to Claims Arising from Fatal Accidents – 2nd Edition' by James Patience
'A Practical Guide to the Ownership of Employee Inventions – From Entitlement to Compensation' by James Tumbridge & Ashley Roughton
'A Practical Guide to Asbestos Claims' by Jonathan Owen & Gareth McAloon
'A Practical Guide to Stamp Duty Land Tax in England and Northern Ireland' by Suzanne O'Hara
'A Practical Guide to the Law of Farming Partnerships' by Philip Whitcomb
'Covid-19, Homeworking and the Law – The Essential Guide to Employment and GDPR Issues' by Forbes Solicitors
'Covid-19 and Criminal Law – The Essential Guide' by Ramya Nagesh

'Covid-19 and Family Law in England and Wales – The Essential Guide' by Safda Mahmood
'A Practical Guide to the Law of Unlawful Eviction and Harassment – 2nd Edition' by Stephanie Lovegrove
'Covid-19, Brexit and the Law of Commercial Leases – The Essential Guide' by Mark Shelton
'A Practical Guide to Costs in Personal Injury Claims – 2nd Edition' by Matthew Hoe
'A Practical Guide to the General Data Protection Regulation (GDPR) – 2nd Edition' by Keith Markham
'Ellis on Credit Hire – Sixth Edition' by Aidan Ellis & Tim Kevan
'A Practical Guide to Working with Litigants in Person and McKenzie Friends in Family Cases' by Stuart Barlow
'Protecting Unregistered Brands: A Practical Guide to the Law of Passing Off' by Lorna Brazell
'A Practical Guide to Secondary Liability and Joint Enterprise Post-Jogee' by Joanne Cecil & James Mehigan
'A Practical Guide to the Pre-Action RTA Claims Protocol for Personal Injury Lawyers' by Antonia Ford
'A Practical Guide to Neighbour Disputes and the Law' by Alexander Walsh
'A Practical Guide to Forfeiture of Leases' by Mark Shelton
'A Practical Guide to Coercive Control for Legal Practitioners and Victims' by Rachel Horman
'A Practical Guide to Rights Over Airspace and Subsoil' by Daniel Gatty
'Tackling Disclosure in the Criminal Courts – A Practitioner's Guide' by Narita Bahra QC & Don Ramble
'A Practical Guide to the Law of Driverless Cars – Second Edition' by Alex Glassbrook, Emma Northey & Scarlett Milligan
'A Practical Guide to TOLATA Claims' by Greg Williams
'A Practical Guide to Elderly Law – 2nd Edition' by Justin Patten
'A Practical Guide to Responding to Housing Disrepair and Unfitness Claims' by Iain Wightwick
'A Practical Guide to the Construction and Rectification of Wills and Trust Instruments' by Edward Hewitt
'A Practical Guide to the Law of Bullying and Harassment in the Workplace' by Philip Hyland

'How to Be a Freelance Solicitor: A Practical Guide to the SRA-Regulated Freelance Solicitor Model' by Paul Bennett
'A Practical Guide to Prison Injury Claims' by Malcolm Johnson
'A Practical Guide to the Small Claims Track - 2nd Edition' by Dominic Bright
'A Practical Guide to Advising Clients at the Police Station' by Colin Stephen McKeown-Beaumont
'A Practical Guide to Antisocial Behaviour Injunctions' by Iain Wightwick
'Practical Mediation: A Guide for Mediators, Advocates, Advisers, Lawyers, and Students in Civil, Commercial, Business, Property, Workplace, and Employment Cases' by Jonathan Dingle with John Sephton
'The Mini-Pupillage Workbook' by David Boyle
'A Practical Guide to Crofting Law' by Brian Inkster
'A Practical Guide to Spousal Maintenance' by Liz Cowell
'A Practical Guide to the Law of Domain Names and Cybersquatting' by Andrew Clemson
'A Practical Guide to the Law of Gender Pay Gap Reporting' by Harini Iyengar
'NHS Whistleblowing and the Law' by Joseph England
'Employment Law and the Gig Economy' by Nigel Mackay & Annie Powell
'A Practical Guide to Noise Induced Hearing Loss (NIHL) Claims' by Andrew Mckie, Ian Skeate, Gareth McAloon
'An Introduction to Beauty Negligence Claims – A Practical Guide for the Personal Injury Practitioner' by Greg Almond
'Intercompany Agreements for Transfer Pricing Compliance' by Paul Sutton
'Zen and the Art of Mediation' by Martin Plowman
'A Practical Guide to the SRA Principles, Individual and Law Firm Codes of Conduct 2019 – What Every Law Firm Needs to Know' by Paul Bennett
'A Practical Guide to Adoption for Family Lawyers' by Graham Pegg
'A Practical Guide to Industrial Disease Claims' by Andrew Mckie & Ian Skeate
'A Practical Guide to Redundancy' by Philip Hyland
'A Practical Guide to Vicarious Liability' by Mariel Irvine
'A Practical Guide to Applications for Landlord's Consent and Variation of Leases' by Mark Shelton
'A Practical Guide to Relief from Sanctions Post-Mitchell and Denton' by Peter Causton

- 'A Practical Guide to Equity Release for Advisors' by Paul Sams
- 'A Practical Guide to Financial Services Claims' by Chris Hegarty
- 'The Law of Houses in Multiple Occupation: A Practical Guide to HMO Proceedings' by Julian Hunt
- 'Occupiers, Highways and Defective Premises Claims: A Practical Guide Post-Jackson – 2nd Edition' by Andrew Mckie
- 'A Practical Guide to Financial Ombudsman Service Claims' by Adam Temple & Robert Scrivenor
- 'A Practical Guide to Advising Schools on Employment Law' by Jonathan Holden
- 'A Practical Guide to Running Housing Disrepair and Cavity Wall Claims: 2nd Edition' by Andrew Mckie & Ian Skeate
- 'A Practical Guide to Holiday Sickness Claims – 2nd Edition' by Andrew Mckie & Ian Skeate
- 'Arguments and Tactics for Personal Injury and Clinical Negligence Claims' by Dorian Williams
- 'A Practical Guide to Drone Law' by Rufus Ballaster, Andrew Firman, Eleanor Clot
- 'A Practical Guide to Compliance for Personal Injury Firms Working With Claims Management Companies' by Paul Bennett
- 'RTA Allegations of Fraud in a Post-Jackson Era: The Handbook – 2nd Edition' by Andrew Mckie
- 'RTA Personal Injury Claims: A Practical Guide Post-Jackson' by Andrew Mckie
- 'On Experts: CPR35 for Lawyers and Experts' by David Boyle
- 'An Introduction to Personal Injury Law' by David Boyle

These books and more are available to order online direct from the publisher at www.lawbriefpublishing.com, where you can also read free sample chapters. For any queries, contact us on 0844 587 2383 or mail@lawbriefpublishing.com.

Our books are also usually in stock at www.amazon.co.uk with free next day delivery for Prime members, and at good legal bookshops such as Wildy & Sons.

We are regularly launching new books in our series of practical day-to-day practitioners' guides. Visit our website and join our free newsletter to be kept informed and to receive special offers, free chapters, etc.

You can also follow us on Twitter at www.twitter.com/lawbriefpub.

www.ingramcontent.com/pod-product-compliance
Lightning Source LLC
LaVergne TN
LVHW052311200926
848481LV00002B/525
9781916698147